The Abuse of Beauty

THE PAUL CARUS LECTURES

PUBLISHED IN MEMORY OF

PAUL CARUS
1852–1919

EDITOR OF
THE OPEN COURT
AND
THE MONIST
FROM
1888 TO 1919

Sublimity Triumphant over Beauty?

With his *Onement I* of 1948, Barnett Newman posed an aesthetic of sublimity against an aesthetic of beauty. "The invention of beauty by the Greeks, . . . their postulate of beauty as an ideal, has been the bugbear of European art and European aesthetic philosophies," Newman wrote. Free from the weight of European culture, a few Americans could now express their relation to the Absolute, undistracted by the pursuit of beauty, the fetishism of perfect quality.

THE PAUL CARUS LECTURE SERIES 21

The Abuse of Beauty

Aesthetics and the Concept of Art

ARTHUR C. DANTO

Open Court
Chicago and La Salle, Illinois

THE PAUL CARUS LECTURE SERIES 21

To order books from Open Court, call toll-free 1-800-815-2280,
or visit our website at www.opencourtbooks.com.

Open Court Publishing Company is a division of Carus Publishing Company.

Printed and bound in the United States of America.

Library of Congress Cataloging-in-Publication Data

Danto, Arthur Coleman, 1924-
        The abuse of beauty : aesthetics and the concept of art / Arthur C. Danto.
            p. cm. — (Paul Carus lectures ; 21st ser.)
        Includes index.
        ISBN 0-8126-9539-9 (alk. paper) — ISBN 0-8126-9540-2 (pbk. : alk. paper)
        1. Aesthetics. 2. Art—Philosophy.   I. Title.   II. Series.
    BH39 .D3489 2003
    111'.85—dc21

                                                                        2003005374

For David Reed and Sean Scully,
as well as to the memory of Robert Motherwell,
and of course for Barbara Westman

Beauty is the promise of happiness

STENDHAL

Contents

Preface

It is a curious fact that while my philosophy of art aspires to the kind of timelessness at which philosophy in general aims, it is so much the product of its historical moment that it can easily be considered to have relevance chiefly to the art that occasioned it. The art itself was the product of various avant-garde art movements of the early 1960s, mainly in and around New York City. Most of the art, moreover, could hardly have been made at a much earlier date. Consider the celebrated *Brillo Box* of Andy Warhol, which has figured so prominently in my thought and writing. It was made and exhibited in 1964, and appropriated the format of a commercial shipping carton, which pre-existed it for little more than a year. The designer of that carton, himself an artist, drew upon stylistic paradigms from contemporary abstract painting. "Brillo" itself was the name of a recently invented soap-pad, held to be particularly effective in brightening aluminum ware. It had only a few years earlier been introduced to the American market. *Brillo Box* could hardly have pre-dated what gave it its meaning. It is possible to imagine that an *object* could have made a century earlier, which resembled it exactly, though it could not have drawn upon the associated meanings that gave life to *Brillo Box* as a work of art. Not merely could the same object not have been the same work of art it was in 1964, it is difficult to see how, in 1864, it could have been a work of art at all. It was difficult enough even in 1964 for many to accept it as art, but by then space had opened up for at least a certain segment of the art world to accept it as art without hesitation. And the question that initially concerned me as a philosopher was what made it possible for something to be a work of art at a given historical moment when it could not have had that status at a much earlier one. At the very least this raised the issue, at the most general philosophical level, of what its historical situation contributes to an object's status as art.

Somehow, the timelessness that belongs to philosophy has tended to inflect the way the objects of philosophical concern are themselves thought of as timeless. But I have always found it philosophically instructive to imagine objects, which are locked into their historical moment the way *Brillo Box* was, transported back to a much earlier time, as Mark Twain famously imagined a Connecticut Yankee conveyed to the court of King Arthur. For the cover of my book, *Beyond the Brillo Box,* the clever painter, Russell Conner, replaced the cadaver with *Brillo Box* in Rembrandt's famous *Anatomy Lesson,* making it appear as if Dr. Tulp's eager seventeenth-century auditors are listening to a discourse on mid-twentieth-century avant-garde art. We are used to the idea of passing from the gallery devoted to seventeenth-century Dutch art to the one dedicated to twentieth-century American art in today's encyclopedic museums. We take in our stride the juxtaposition of works from various centuries and cultures in a single gallery, in which they are allowed to "communicate" with one another, as curators like to say. But those for whom Rembrandt painted would have had no way of accommodating *Brillo Box* under their concept of art. In 1917, Marcel Duchamp undertook to enter an "assisted readymade"—in effect a urinal—into an exhibition which was to have had no jury, where it was rejected by the hanging committee on the explicit grounds that it was not art. There were sectors of the 1917 art world hospitable to Duchamp's ready-mades, but the hanging committee of the Society of Independent Artists, which sponsored the exhibition, was clearly not part of it. In much the same way, there were large parts of the artworld of 1964 for which *Brillo Box* was not art. But there were not and could not have been any parts of the artworld of Paris in 1864—or Amsterdam in 1664—in which *Brillo Box* could have fitted. It is true, of course, that the concept of art was beginning to loosen up sufficiently that Manet's *Déjeuner sur l'herbe* was accepted as art in 1864, though for most who had seen it in the recent *Salon des refuses* it was a perversion of the very idea of art. Heinrich Wollflin wrote that not everything is possible at every time. In that sense of historical impossibility, *Brillo Box,* while just possible as an object, was not possible as art much before the moment it was made. (One has to remember that *Brillo Box* was made of industrial plywood, which may not have existed in 1864, let alone 1664, and was painted with silkscreen ink, which almost certainly did not. Philosophers

FIGURE 1 Russell Conner, *Cover image for* Beyond the Brillo Box
Content may be lost in temporal transit.

are exceedingly casual when they perform such "thought experiments." An object like that in which *Brillo Box* consists might have elicited astonishment, much in the way in which coconut shells did when they washed ashore in medieval Europe.)

These considerations throw some doubt not only on the timelessness of art, but, in a more immediate way, put in question how works of art are to be approached critically and aesthetically. It must be an assumption of formalism, as a critical approach, that everything relevant to addressing a work of art must be present and accessible at every moment of the work's existence. There is, so to say, a position in the philosophy of art analogous to Internalism in the philosophies of mind and of meaning. Works of art, of course, change physically over time, sometimes in radical ways—pigments fade, statues lose appendages like arms and legs. And information relevant to the identification and interpretation of a work is sometimes simply forgotten: we no longer know the identity of persons in old portraits; the individuals who knew the keys to reading certain signs and symbols have died without passing that knowledge on to others. We simply don't know how to read Pieter Breugel's prints the way his contemporaries, or some of them, presumably could. There are words whose only known occurrence in English is in one of Shakespeare's plays, so that if the manuscript were missing, even specialists would have no way of knowing what the missing words were. The relationship between the play and the manuscript is metaphysically delicate, but certainly not a matter of strict identity. So the changes that works of art as physical objects undergo are really merely contingent. It is with reference to the work of art, to the degree that it can be distinguished from the physical object, that one refers when one says that nothing outside it is relevant to understanding it critically and aesthetically. Internalism in art is the position that everything relevant to appreciation is ideally available to the critic's eye at any moment, and nothing beyond that is relevant to experiencing the art as art.

It is the work of art in this curious sense, as distinct from the physical object, that I am imagining transferred to some earlier historical moment—*Brillo Box* as a kind of formal design. But what will have been lost in this imagined transit is what I have spoken of here as the meanings that give the work life. For meaning is based on art's connection to the world, and the relations between the design and the world are historical. The name "Brillo," for example, designates a household product, invented and patented at a certain time. Before that, it was just a noise, or, a written design—or at best a word in some form of dog Latin. On *Brillo Box*, there is a mark that consists of a circle with a "u" inscribed in the center. This is a logo used to mean that the product that bears it is certified as kosher by the Union of Orthodox Rabbis in Jerusalem, which was established after the state of Israel came into being. Brillo was kosher in 1964, but is kosher no longer, so the Brillo cartons in the supermarkets are no longer entitled to display the logo. Is the logo part of the design or not? This is something I shall leave to formalists to worry about. A much more important consideration is the fact that, as already stated, *Brillo Box* itself, as a work, stands in the relationship of "appropriation of" to the cartons in which Brillo was shipped from factories to distributors and thence to supermarkets from the mid-sixties until the late 1990s, when the design of the cartons changed. But even more important than that, the interest and importance of *Brillo Box* is very much bound up with attitudes toward art that prevailed in art in early to mid 1960s, especially in Manhattan. Part of what made it possible for it to be art at the time was the fact that this atmosphere of history and of theory defined what was historically possible. In 1964, when I published "The Art World" in the *Journal of Philosophy*—the text in which the first outlines of my philosophy of art were laid out—my thought was that, in order to see *Brillo Box* as art, one would have had to have known something of the history, and something of the theory that defined the relevant art world of that moment. There were many art worlds, even in New York, at that particular moment. I don't want to relativize art to art worlds, but only at this point to emphasize that *Brillo Box*'s status as artwork depended upon external factors which were not in place much earlier than 1964.

I want to say something about the degree to which these historical considerations belong to the concept of art, but I had better interject a few words about the concept of concepts itself. It has often been noted that the Greeks, with whom the philosophy of art began in the west, did not have a word for art in their vocabulary. But they certainly had a concept of art, which included in its extension a great many of the same kinds of objects we would consider works of art today. A definition of art that excluded Greek sculpture or Greek dramas would ipso facto be unacceptable. At the same time, they were aware that certain properties, characteristic of these objects, were not part of the concept of art, even if they were widely present. I refer in the first instance to mimetic properties: Greek statuary was believed to resemble its subjects, in much the same way that Greek tragedies were believed to resemble certain historical episodes in the lives of their heroes. The technique of resemblance indeed defined a progressive history in the main mimetic arts that have come down to us—sculpture and drama. It was a progress defined in the direction of life-likeness, from archaic figures of Apollo to figures so close to the way human beings look that there was a genuine possibility of illusion. This possibility must have played an important role in Greek forms of life, especially in religious worship, where statues of gods and goddesses were so compelling that one might believe oneself in the very presence of the deities themselves, especially in the dark, smoky atmosphere of temple interiors. In Nietzsche's account of early tragedy, there was a moment in which the central actor was believed by celebrants actually to be possessed by a god, so that the chorus could feel that Dionysus, for example, was there among them. It is not implausible to suppose something like this could have been believed of statues of the gods in temples dedicated to their cult. After all, the "mystical presence of the saint in the icon" has been widely subscribed to in Greek Orthodoxy, where it played a central role in the fierce iconoclastic controversies of eighth-century Byzantium. There was no implication that artistic quality was indexed to differing degrees of life-likeness—no sense that Aeschylus was Euripides's inferior. So Socrates, in his famous polemic, was able to imply that life-likeness was no part of the *concept* of art, though widely prized in his own age. It was, however, central to the Greeks' concept that art should represent things. But degrees of life-likeness in mimetic representation were matters in part of taste, in part of function, and it was clear to Plato that there were modes of representation other than mimesis, whatever degree of life-likeness the latter might have. Their notion of representation was fairly abstract and general. And so of course is mine, when I have proposed representation as part of the definition of art. I emphasized representation in considering how one would distinguish as art something that deeply resembles something that is not art at all. My concern was occasioned by the art of the 1960s, but it is meant as universal and timeless.

Here is another example. From the eighteenth century to early in the twentieth century, it was the presumption that art should possess beauty. This was so much the case that beauty would have been among the first things people would think of in connection with—well—*les beaux-arts*. When Roger Fry organized his great exhibitions of Post-Impressionist art at the Grafton Gallery in London, in 1910 and 1912, the public was outraged not only by the disregard of life-likeness, which characterized so much of the modernist movement, but by the palpable absence of beauty. In his defense, Fry argued that the new art would be seen as ugly *until* it was seen as beautiful. To see it as beautiful, he implied, requires aesthetic education, and that the beauty would be seen in the course of time. Undoubtedly we sometimes do come to see beauty that evaded us at first—but suppose we don't? Is it because we are blind to the beauty—or is it because we have wrongly taken it as a given that art *must* be beautiful? What I shall speak of in this book as the Intractable Avant-garde abjured beauty. I mean in the first instance Dada, which refused to make beautiful objects for the gratification of those they held responsible for the Great War. In his Dialogues with Cabanne, Duchamp is dismissive of the whole idea of what he calls "the retinal flutter," which art since Courbet was suppose to induce in viewers. He was keen on an intellectual art, with no sensory gratification whatever. I regard the Intractable Avant-garde as having taken an immense philosophical step forward. It helped show that beauty was no part of the concept of art, that beauty could be present or not, and something still be art. The concept of art may require the presence of one or another from a range of features, which includes beauty, but includes a great many others as well, such as sublimity, to use another feature much discussed in the eighteenth century. For the moment, I'll call these *pragmatic*, to contrast with the *semantical* ones, which mimesis exemplifies, borrowing this vocabulary from Charles Morris's Theory of Signs, which played an important role in the heyday of Logical Positivism. Pragmatic properties are intended to dispose an audience to have feelings of one sort or another toward what the artwork represents. Morris says in passing that what he calls pragmatism was called rhetoric in earlier times, and rhetoric was one of the defining disciplines of the classical age. It may be the pragmatic function of beauty to inspire love toward what an artwork shows, and the function of sublimity to inspire awe. But there are a great many other cases, such as disgust, to inspire revulsion, or ludicrousness, to inspire contempt. Or lubricity, to arouse erotic feelings. In a way, pragmatic properties correspond to what Frege speaks of as "color"— *Farbung*—in his theory of meaning.

The range of pragmatic features is far wider than anything really compassed by the canon of writings in aesthetics, just as the range of semantic features includes far more than mimetic representations. But my concern here is simply to have picked out a few of the components that figure, or could figure, in the conceptual analysis of art, and to make clear how narrowly that concept has been construed in the philosophical and critical literature devoted to art. A philosophical definition of art has to be cast in the most general terms, in order for everything that has ever or could ever have been a work of art to be covered by it. It has to be general enough to be immune to counter-examples. And while I cannot pretend that I have achieved a formulation that meets such a condition, that is what has governed my philosophy of art as an undertaking from the beginning. But it is precisely that which dealing with the art of the mid-sixties has made possible. For that was a period in which so much that had been felt part of the concept of art had fallen out of consideration entirely. Not merely beauty and mimesis, but almost everything that had figured in the life of art had been erased. The definition of art would have to be built on the ruins of what had been thought to be the concept of art in previous discourses. This returns me to my paradigm.

The issue which concerned me immediately in connection with *Brillo Box* was not simply what made it art, but how, if it was a work of art, objects exactly (or exactly enough) like it were not, namely the multitude of cartons designed for the transport of Brillo pads. It doubtless belongs to the interpretation of this segment of Warhol's oeuvre that it uses logos from commercial art for purposes of art. But in truth, Warhol could have made art of anything, so long as what he made it of belonged to the domain of objects that were not works of art. In 1964, he used, for example, police photographs of "Most Wanted" criminals, as well as newspaper photographs of plane crashes, suicides, and automobile accidents. There is something we can speak of as Warhol's "style," which determined which, among the vast number of things he could have made art of, he did make art of. All that I required of his art, however, was that there should exist examples of things that were not art, so long as they and the art should look as much alike as *Brillo Box* looked like the ordinary Brillo boxes. This gave me the idea of indiscernible pairs, one of which was an art work and the other not, so that I could then ask on what basis one of each pair should be an artwork and the other just a thing. This turned out to be a powerful tool for the conceptual research I needed. But it hardly suggested itself as a tool much before the possibility actually existed in artistic practice.

Now in truth, I could have found examples of these pairs everywhere in the art world of the 1960s. *Fluxus*, for example, used food as art. Minimalists used sections of prefabricated buildings and other industrial products. Pop artists like Lichtenstein enlarged the cartoons on the inside of bubblegum wrappers, and presented them as paintings. The Conceptualist Dennis Oppenheim dug a hole in a mountain near Oakland, California, and offered it as a sculpture which could not be transported to a museum. By 1969, the Conceptualists were ready to consider everything as art, and were prepared to consider anyone an artist, much the way that Joseph Beuys was shortly to propose. Examples could be found in dance, especially in the Judson Group, where it was possible for a dance to consist in someone sitting in a chair; and in avant-garde music, which challenged the distinction between musical and non-musical sounds. The 1960s avant-garde was interested in overcoming the gap between life and art. It was interested in erasing the distinction between fine and vernacular art. But by time the decade was over, there was very little left of what anyone would earlier have thought was part of the concept of art. It was a period of spectacular philosophical erasure. Bliss was it in that dawn to be alive!

There can be no question that my philosophy was itself very much part of that moment, though I was aware only of part of what was taking place, and even more is it the case that none of those in the artworld—or in the set of overlapping artworlds of the time—were aware of my philosophy at all. Only recently has the 1964 "The Art World" begun to appear in anthologies of documents for the art history of those years. But the structures with which I was working were very much those of analytical philosophy. My book, *Analytical Philosophy of History* was in press in 1964, and the ideas of that book inflected the way I thought about everything. In that book, for example, I argued, through a kind of truth-condition analysis, that the meanings of historical events are invisible to those who live through them. That was the Externalist kind of thesis that I followed in the analysis of the concept of an artwork—that what makes an object an artwork is external to it.

But let us return to the philosophical situation of that moment in art. Once one reflects on what made that moment so unique, two things have to become clear. The first is that, once it is seen that anything can be an artwork, there is little point in asking whether this or that can be artworks, since the answer will always be yes. They may not be works of art, but they can be. So the second thing is that the question now became urgent of what must be the case if they *are* to be works of art. That means that a theory of art is all at once imperative in a way that it had never appeared to be before. It is also transparent that no previous theory of art could be of great help, since none had been formulated in the kind of situation that defined the art world of the 1960s, namely, that in which anything, however banal, could be a work of art. One could only achieve the generality that philosophy demands against the extreme latitude that the sixties made vivid. So it was a great time to be a philosopher of art.

My own work in this marvelous field has been inspired by two interconnected thoughts of Hegel. The first is his thought that the philosophy suited to a form of life can only properly begin when that form of life has grown old: "When philosophy paints its gray in gray, then has a form of life grown old," he writes, elegaically, in *The Philosophy of Right*. I think that only when the history of art comes to its end can the philosophy of art fully begin. It can do so because, until then, philosophy does not have all the pieces it needs to build the theory. But that connects with the second thought I have, based in a way on Hegel's masterpiece, *The Phenomenology of Spirit*. That book has the structure, as the American philosopher, Josiah Royce once suggested, of a *Bildungsroman*. Spirit, or *Geist*, as Hegel terms his subject, undergoes in the course of the book the education through which it comes to discover its own identity. That is the kind of *Bildung* that Hegel was concerned with, and that we are all concerned with in coming through experience to learn what we really are. I like to think of the history of art as a *Bildungsroman* in this way as well, in which *Kunst* discovers bit by bit *its* own identity. Philosophy is the changing consciousness of this history in the sense that at each stage, a piece of the puzzle emerges which philosophy supposes is what *Kunst* is. But, as with the *Phenomenology*, this is often partial and often wrong. It is not a smooth progress. *Kunst*'s adventures, peradventures, and misadventures, make up not the history of art, which has been the province of art history as a discipline, but *the philosophical history of art*, which in effect is the history of the philosophy of art. That history reached a new level in the 1960s when it at last became clear that everything was possible as art. The end of art, as I have used that phrase, means this. It is now possible to give an answer to the question of *Kunst*'s identity which we know cannot be overthrown by the further history of art. That is what must be true of every philosophical definition.

In this preface, I have mentioned two conditions which help specify that identity. One of them is that to be art, it must represent something, that is, it must have some semantic property. A good bit of my book, *The Transfiguration of the Commonplace* is addressed to establishing this. I would like to say that having some of what I have here called pragmatic features is a second condition, but I am not sure this would be true. I am not because I am uncertain what role if any pragmatic properties play in the art of today. They have, however, played an overwhelming part in the art of the past, and were held to give an answer to the question, were anyone to ask it, of what the point of art is.

If I am of my own historical moment, that would explain why I have neglected to raise, let alone attempt to answer this question, and in the fact that I have rarely considered in the analysis of art the role if any of beauty and the like. This in part is to be explained by the historical circumstances under which my philosophy of art originated: the avant-garde art of the 1960s turned its back on aesthetics almost as resolutely as the avant-garde philosophy of that period turned its back on edification. Both aspired to be "cool." I think this was, in the philosophy of art, a healthy move. It helped separate the philosophy of art from aesthetics, which has always been such a muddle. I think we have now built up sufficient immunities that we can again consider what after all makes art so meaningful in human life, and that is my current agenda. Protected by what I have learned, I can begin once again to pick up, with the long forceps of analytical philosophy, such toxic properties as beauty, sublimity, and the like. There are probably good reasons why beauty has been the paradigm pragmatic property in the history of art, and its entrenchment in the discourse more than justifies the emphasis I shall assign it in this book.

When I began to think through the project of framing a definition of art, the philosophy of art was dominated by two main theses: that no such definition was possible, and that no such definition was needed. The latter was largely a Wittgensteinian response to the former. But as so often with Wittgenstein, his position presupposed a stability in the set of things called by a given term—in this instance "work of art"—so the speakers of the language can be expected in general to recognize instances of art works for the most part. The former position, meanwhile, was based on the immense pluralism that was beginning to prevail in art: so many things became possible as works of art that no definition seemed any longer possible. The conservatism of the Wittgensteinian view was beginning to be threatened almost at the moment it was enunciated. What we now know is that only when the radical pluralism was registered in consciousness was a definition finally possible. It must consist in properties which must always be present, however various the class of artworks turns out to be—as in the Whitney Biennial of 2002 for example. That pluralism was evidently not discernible even as late as when Wittgenstein's philosophy began to be applied to the philosophy of art by his followers. Only when pluralism itself becomes established is it finally possible to do the philosophy of art in a transhistorical way. So one can aim at last at a timeless philosophy of art only at a moment like the present one, which is after all unique in the history of art. Only by paying the closest attention to the art of my historical moment, have I been able to hope for a philosophy of art valid for all historical moments.

This brings me to a third thought of Hegel's. We are all children of our times, he writes—but it is the task of philosophers to grasp their times as thought. Since the 1960s, and compulsively since the 1980s, I have tried to turn my experiences in the art world into philosophy. One can only do that if one lives the times in question, and that makes this book more personal and confessional than philosophy is expected to be, and more abstract than confessions commonly are. There is a tradition of meditative confession in the literature of philosophy, but mainly one must not regard this book as pretending to any kind of scholarly authority. Its authority, if it has any, lies elsewhere. I have dispensed with footnotes, which, except in the most scholarly of writing on art, constitute a *façade* of craved authority. Read it as an adventure story, with a few philosophical arguments and distinctions as trophies brought back from my encounters with the life of art in our times.

ARTHUR C. DANTO
New York City, 2002

Acknowledgments

The Paul Carus Lectures, named after the editor of *The Open Court*, the Open Court Publishing Company, and *The Monist*, are sponsored by the Foundation established in his memory. Generally, the lecturer is invited to present a series of three lectures at a meeting of one or another of the three divisions of the American Philosophical Association, and at three-year intervals. The series I know best is C.I. Lewis's 1946 *An Analysis of Knowledge and Valuation,* which I read as a graduate student, and which, for better or worse, defined the way I thought and in many ways still think, not only about the theory of knowledge but almost everything else. Lewis's was the Seventh Series—the first was John Dewey's *Experience and Nature*—and both of these are far too substantial as volumes to represent a mere three lectures. It is understood that the lectures are to be published as a book by Open Court, but that means that the manuscript will finally contain a fair amount of material not in the lectures themselves. And so it is in the present case. Nothing can be considered a book that lacks a spine, and three one-hour lectures, bound together, is at best little more than a pamphlet.

The three lectures that I delivered under the title *The Revolt Against Beauty* at what turned out to be the 100th Anniversary of the American Philosophical Association on December 26–28, 2001, in Atlanta, Georgia, correspond to Chapters 1, 2, and 4 of this book, though much expanded, and in the case of Chapter 4 radically altered. Chapter 3, "Beauty and Beautification," is a greatly modified version of a contribution to Peg Brand's anthology, *Beauty Matters* (Bloomington: Indiana University Press, 1998), refitted to the context of the Carus Lectures. Chapter 2 borrows from my review of an exhibition of Paul McCarthy, which appeared in *The Nation,* 23 April, 2001, as well as from a response to an argument by Jean Clair, "Marcel Duchamp and the End of Taste: A Defense of Contemporary Art,*"* which appears in English in *Tout-fait: The Marcel Duchamp Studies On-line Journal* 1, 3, www.tout-fait.com, but otherwise only in Dutch translation as "Marcel Duchamp en her einde van de smaak: een apologie van de moderne kunst." *Nexus* 27: 199–217. I am grateful to the Nexus Institute for inviting my response to Jean Clair, which opened up the concept of disgust for me in valuable ways.

Chapter 5, "Beauty and Politics" draws some of its language from "Beauty and Morality," which was delivered as a keynote address at the conference, "Whatever Happened to Beauty?" held at the University of Texas at Austin, and published in my *Embodied Meanings: Critical Essays and Asesthetic Meditations* (New York: Farrar, Straus, Giroux, 1994). Chapter 6 is almost unrecognizably different from "The Museum as Will-to-Power," presented at a conference on the museum at Skidmore College and published in *Salmagundi*. An adaptation of Chapter 7 was presented as "The American Sublime," in a conference organized by the University of Ghent under the title "Shadows of the the Sublime," in October 2002. My preface draws on an Afterword, written especially for a collection of my writings that appeared in Dutch translation, under the title *De Komedie van de Overeen-komsten,* edited by Frank Ankersmit and Wessel Krul (Groningen: Historische Uitgeverij, 2002). And the Introduction was inspired by a preface especially written for the Spanish translation of *Beyond the Brillo Box.*

I am grateful in the first instance to the American Philosophical Association, which selected me as the Carus Lecturer for 2001; and to Open Court Publishing Company for sponsoring the lectures and for publishing the book which grew out of them. It meant a great deal to me that Richard Rorty, Peg Brand, and Noel Carroll agreed to introduce the three sessions at which the lectures were delivered, but to Peg Brand I owe a particular debt for having encouraged me to write on the topic of beauty in the first instance. David Ramsay Steele, editor at Open Court, subtly encouraged me to ready the book rather earlier than I might have, which was all to the good. My marvelous wife and companion, the artist Barbara Westman, blesses my life. Her unfailing cheerfulness, humor, love, and high spirits are the elixir that explains my happiness and productivity.

David Carrier, and then Richard and Margaret Kuhns read the lectures before they were delivered, and I am obliged to them for their comments, and grateful for their friendship and love. After the lectures were presented, I sent copies to a number of friends, artists and others, eager to have their responses, which greatly encouraged me to go on to the larger project of this book. I particularly thank David Reed, Robert Mangold, Sean Scully, Robert Zakanitch, George and Betty Woodman, Frank Ankersmit, Michael Kelly, Karlheinz Lüdeking, Jonathan Gilmore, Fred Rush Jr., Lydia Goehr, Mary Mothersill, Bill Berkson, James Ackerman, Amelie Rorty, and John Perrault for their thoughts. Martha Nussbaum's enthusiasm for the lectures and for this project meant an immense amount.

Various stages of my thought on this topic were worked out during my residences at the Acadia Summer Program in the Arts, on Mt. Desert Island in Maine, which exists through the generosity and imagination of the remarkable Kippy Stroud. In dedicating an earlier essay to Kippy, I wrote that The Acadian Summer Program in the Arts is the closest to Duino Castle the United States affords. She is the Princess of Thurn und Taxis: it is not her fault that her guests from the art world are not all Rilkes! Barbara and I cherish her as a person and as a friend, and the present book is but one of the many things she has helped make possible.

Acknowledgments for Illustrations

Illustrations in this book appear by permission. Cover image: *L.H.O.O.Q* (Replica of, from Boite-en-Valise) by Marcel Duchamp (1950-134-934). Philadelphia Museum of Art: The Louise and Walter Arensberg Collection. Reproduced by permission; Frontispiece: *Vir Heroicus Sublimis* by Barnett Newman, © Estate of Barnett Newman, Digital image © The Museum of Modern Art/Licensed by SCALA / Art Resource, NY.

Valoche: A Flux Travel Aid by George Brecht, Collection Walker Art Center, Minneapolis, Walker Special Purchase Fund, 1989; ARS (Artists Rights Society) for *Woman with Hat* and *Blue Nude* by Henri Matisse, © 2003 Succession H. Matisse, Paris / Artists Rights Society (ARS), New York; The Baltimore Museum of Art: The Cone Collection, formed by Dr. Claribel Cone and Miss Etta Cone of Baltimore, Maryland, BMA 1950.228, for *Blue Nude (Souvenir de Biskra)* by Henri Matisse; Damien Hirst / Science Ltd for *A Thousand Years* by Damien Hirst; the photograph of *Expanded Expansion* by Eva Hesse is reproduced with the permission of the Estate of Eva Hesse, Galerie Hauser & Wirth, Zurich; SFMOMA (San Francisco Museum of Modern Art) for *Femme au chapeau (Woman with Hat)* by Henri Matisse; Daniel Joseph Martinez for *Museum Tags: Second Movement (Overture)* or *Overture con Claque—Overture with Hired Audience Members* by Daniel Joseph Martinez, courtesy The Project Gallery, New York; VAGA (Visual Artists and Galleries Association, Inc.) for *Elegy for the Spanish Republic #172* by Robert Motherwell; David McKee for *The Studio* by Philip Guston, © Estate of Philip Guston; Museum of Art, Rhode Island School of Design, Mary B. Jackson Fund, for *The Wedding of Peleus and Thetis* by Joachim Wtewael; *Onement I* and *Vir Heroicus Sublimis*, © Estate of Barnett Newman, Digital images © The Museum of Modern Art / Licensed by SCALA / Art Resource, NY.

INTRODUCTION

The Aesthetics of Brillo Boxes

Art is for aesthetics what the birds are for ornithology.

TESTADURA

I was required, as a graduate student of philosophy in Columbia University at the beginning of the 1950s, to become sufficiently conversant with the literature of aesthetics to pass an examination, qualifying me to teach the subject in the unlikely event of finding an academic position. I found the readings interesting but largely irrelevant, since I was never able to see what they had to do with the art that had brought me to New York in the first place. It was not that aesthetic considerations, in a larger sense, were irrelevant to the culture of Abstract Expressionism: they were, rather, central in the endless discussions that took place about the exciting painting that one went to see in the galleries that showed this work, or wrangled over at artists' parties. It was just that nothing I had learned about in the canonical aesthetic texts seemed remotely connected with what was happening in the art. The questions that exercised the painters I knew seemed so distant from the philosophy that claimed to touch upon art that one who knew both sides of the matter had to wonder what the point of the philosophy was. It was long after the occasion on which he first said it that I heard a version of the celebrated putdown of aesthetics by the witty and truculent artist, Barnett Newman— "Aesthetics is for art what ornithology is for the birds."—but it seemed to put into a nutshell the frustrating disconnection between the two sides of my life.

It rather pained me to learn that Newman's particular target was my teacher, and later my friend, Susanne K. Langer, in a panel convened to discuss "Aesthetics and the Artist" at Woodstock, New York, in August, 1952, the year I was appointed to an instructorship at Columbia. The form of the putdown reflected a certain *esprit d'escalier.* What Newman had actually said was that he had never encountered an ornithologist who thought what he was doing was "for the birds," which was a wicked *double entendre,* given the vernacular use of that expression. But perhaps Newman sensed that the theme of the panel really did imply a somewhat patronizing picture of the artists learning from some aesthetician what they were really doing—as if the birds were to take notes from the ornithologists on what it meant to be a bird. If that was the intention of the panel, what aesthetic knowledge it could have been from which the artists might have learned something about being artists, remains to this day closed to me.

Meanwhile, the overall attitude among analytical philosophers, with whom I aligned myself, was that aesthetics itself was for the birds. It was just not something "real" philosophers did. So for some years aesthetics languished in a kind of no-man's-land between philosophy and art, which meant that I was able to live the two parts of my life as if they had nothing much to do with one another, writing analytical philosophy with one hand, as it were, and painting with the other. When I came to write my first piece in the philosophy of art in 1964, I modeled it on the kind of thinking that characterized the philosophy of science and the theory of language that defined "respectable" philosophy at the time. Abstract Expressionism was giving way, in the early 1960s, to a movement—really to a set of movements—so entirely at odds with its attitudes and spirit that one felt one had entered a new and even a revolutionary moment in the history of art. But it was a moment in which it at last seemed to me that it was possible to think philosophically about art, and even that it was now necessary to do so. Unlike Abstract Expressionism, in which aesthetics as a form of lived experience—as distinct from aesthetics as a philosophical discipline—was so central to its being as art, the brash and irreverent art of the early 1960s seemed to have no room for aesthetics at all. It was as if it and analytical philosophy were made for one another.

Both were indifferent to edification and exaltation, both appealed to a kind of hard-edge thinking. It was for me a particularly exhilarating moment. I would have had no interest in being an artist in the new period. But I found it intoxicating to be a philosopher of art when art had shuffled off all the heavy metaphysical draperies the Abstract Expressionists were happy to wear as their intellectual garments, and were content to produce works that looked for all the world like commonplace objects of daily life.

Pop art was among other things an effort to overcome the division between fine and vernacular art—between the exalted and the coarse, the high and the low—where the latter was exemplified by the imagery of comic strips or the logos of commercial art. I had in particular been overwhelmed by a 1964 exhibition I have since written about extensively—and perhaps obsessively—in which Andy Warhol displayed a large number of wooden boxes painted to resemble the cartons in which Brillo pads were packed and shipped from their place of manufacture to the stores in which they were sold. I was struck by the question of how it was possible for Warhol's boxes to be works of art while their counterparts in everyday life were but utilitarian containers with no artistic pretensions whatever. Aesthetics seemed to bear on this issue not at all, since the two sets of boxes, which seemed to have distinct philosophical identities, so resembled one another that it seemed scarcely credible that one of them should have aesthetic qualities the other lacked. So aesthetics simply dropped out of the equation, and never particularly figured in the extensive philosophical literature my 1964 essay, titled "The Art World," engendered.

I have, however, recently come to think that aesthetics did have a certain role to play in the fact that it was with specific reference to the Brillo Boxes that I framed my question. For those were not the only boxes that Warhol showed on that occasion. As I remember the exhibition, Warhol simulated five or six different cartons: Kellogg's Corn Flakes, Delmonte Peach Halves, Heinz Ketchup, Campbell's Tomato Juice, in addition to Brillo. All these boxes were made of plywood, with their commonplace logos stenciled onto their surfaces. And like *Brillo Box*, these boxes looked very like their counterparts in commercial life, though the latter were customarily made of corrugated cardboard. They were like enough, in any case, to raise for me the question that came to occupy my philosophical passion for some time—why were

Warhol's boxes works of art, to be recorded in the *catalogue raisonné* of his work and displayed as sculptures in countless exhibitions, while the boxes in the supermarket were just paper containers, to be used for endless utilitarian purposes—for storage or as second-hand mailing containers, or bundled up to be recycled as waste-paper? There were of course differences between the commercial cartons and Warhol's "sculptures"—but the differences seemed too trivial for the philosophical purpose of distinguishing art from reality.

Now these questions could have been raised with *any* of the boxes in the show. Why was *Brillo Box* somehow the fulcrum I used for lifting the issue that was to form the foundation of my philosophy of art? I think it had to have been because it was somehow visually outstanding, which is what one would expect from a piece of successful commercial art, as the original Brillo carton was. But this was not something Warhol was responsible for. It was, I subsequently was to discover, a part-time package designer named James Harvey who came up with the wonderful design. Harvey was a somewhat tragic figure—an exceptionally promising Abstract Expressionist painter, who had to earn his living as a commercial artist, just as Warhol himself had had to do, but who died too early to fulfill his promise. I have seen a photograph of Harvey, holding his Brillo box while kneeling in front of one of the large and energetic paintings that had already earned him a certain reputation as an artist with great expectations. As it is, he is quite forgotten today. But I owe him a great deal, for he is the one who conceived that brilliant design, so urgent and contemporary, that caught my eye nearly forty years ago. Of course, Warhol had the genius to make art out of what looked like the most banal of everyday objects in consumer culture. But would the question that obsessed me ever have been raised had it not been for Harvey's achievement as a prodigy of commercial design? I think Warhol himself owes something to James Harvey as well. It is difficult to know what the impact on art world consciousness would have been, had his show of boxes consisted only of *Brillo Box*'s relatively drab peers—the Kellogg's Corn Flake box, for example, or the buff brown container for tomato ketchup. *Brillo Box* made the show an instant success. It, rather than any of the other boxes, were featured in a famous photograph by Fred McDarrah, which shows the artist, standing like a

FIGURE 2 James Harvey holding his Brillo carton, 1964
A prodigy of commercial design

stockroom clerk, pale and pasty-faced, surrounded by what, though works of art, could have been simple packing cases full of Brillo. The Brillo Boxes were, thanks to James Harvey, the star of the show and have gone on since to become stars of art history. And it is aesthetics that explains their glamour, even if Warhol himself had nothing to do with that.

My singling out *Brillo Box* for philosophical attention was one of the countless decisions all of us make at every moment of our lives, based on differences in aesthetic appeal. It is a good example of how design compels choice—makes us reach for one product rather than for one of its competitors instead, whether we are picking out a soap pad or a necktie or, for the matter, an oil painting. Part of the success of Pop Art as a world movement was that its practitioners appropriated the achievements of often nameless designers, initially made in order to lend products a certain edge in the ruthless struggle for market advantage. The dissident artists, Vitaly Komar and Alexandre Malamud told me that they discovered Pop Art from seeing it in half-tone illustrations in various art magazines that had a clandestine circulation in the Soviet Union, and appropriated its strategies for their own subversive purposes in a movement they called "Zotz Art." One result of *Glasnost* was the ceremonial exchange of art exhibitions, which is one of the ways in which nations symbolically express friendship for one another; and the Zotz artists could scarcely contain their excitement when a show of American Pop Art in Moscow was announced. What they were unprepared for, Alex Malamud remembers, was how *beautiful* Pop Art was! But that was to be credited entirely to commercial artists, with their use of intense colors and simple forms and smooth outlines—all those aesthetic strategies that, as Warhol once said, the Abstract Expressionists would not look at twice. The extent to which America's victory in the Cold War can be credited to the aesthetics of American commercial art can hardly be exaggerated. The image of all those gay packages densely arrayed on supermarket shelves made the sparse dreary shelves of government dispensaries insupportable.

The Disappearance of Beauty

It is a matter of some irony in my own case that while the aesthetics of Pop Art opened art up for me to philosophical analysis, aesthetics itself has until now had little to contribute to my philosophy of art. That in part is because my interests have largely been in the philosophical definition of art. The issue of defining art became urgent in the twentieth century when art works began to appear which looked like ordinary objects, as in the notorious case of Marcel Duchamp's readymades. As with the Brillo boxes of

Andy Warhol and James Harvey, aesthetics could not explain why one was a work of fine art and the other not, since for all practical purposes they were aesthetically indiscernible: if one was beautiful, the other one had to be beautiful, since they looked just alike. So aesthetics simply disappeared from what Continental philosophers call the "problematic" of defining art. I must admit this may have been an artifact of the way I set about addressing the problem. Still, aesthetics had been too closely associated with art since it first became a topic for philosophy in ancient times to be entirely disregarded in a definition. And as my experience with the *Brillo Box* demonstrates, the aesthetics of artworks has a place in an account of why they please us, even if it is not much different from the way aesthetics functions in everyday choices—in selecting garments or choosing sexual partners or picking a dog out of a litter or an apple out of a display of apples. There is doubtless a psychology of everyday aesthetics to be worked out, and if there are what one might call laws of aesthetic preference, it would be greatly to our advantage to learn what they are. Intuitively, apple merchants polish pieces of fruit, and give prominence to especially well-formed items. And everyone knows the way cosmetics are employed to make ourselves look more desirable—to make the eyes look larger and the hair shinier and fuller and the lips redder and more moist. But is that the way it is with the aesthetics of works of art? To make them look more attractive to collectors? Or has it some deeper role to play in the meaning of art?

The philosophical conception of aesthetics was almost entirely dominated by the idea of beauty, and this was particularly the case in the eighteenth century—the great age of aesthetics—when apart from the sublime, the beautiful was the only aesthetic quality actively considered by artists and thinkers. And yet beauty had almost entirely disappeared from artistic reality in the twentieth century, as if attractiveness was somehow a stigma, with its crass commercial implications. Aesthetics, as I said at the beginning of this introduction, was the very substance of artistic experience in Abstract Expressionist culture. But what made paintings "work" seemed poorly captured by the way beauty had been classically formulated, with reference to balance and proportion and order. "Beautiful!" itself just became an expression of generalized approbation, with as little descriptive content as a whistle someone might emit in the presence of something that especially wowed them. So it was no great loss to the discourse of art when the early Logical Positivists came to think of beauty as bereft of cognitive meaning altogether. To speak of something as beautiful, on their view, is not to describe it, but to express one's overall admiration. And this could be done by just saying "Wow"—or rolling one's eyes and pointing to it. Beyond what was dismissed as its "emotive meaning," the idea of beauty appeared to be cognitively void—and that in part accounted for the vacuity of aesthetics as a discipline, which had banked so heavily on beauty as its central concept. In any case it seemed to have so little to do with what art had become in the latter part of the century that what philosophical interest art held could be addressed without needing to worry overmuch about it—or without needing to worry about it at all.

Another Look at Beauty

Things began to change somewhat in the 1990s. Beauty was provocatively declared to be the defining problem of the decade by the widely admired art-writer Dave Hickey, and this was hailed as an exciting thought. My sense is that it was exciting less because of beauty itself, than because beauty was proxy for something that had almost disappeared from most of one's encounters with art, namely enjoyment and pleasure. In 1993 when Hickey's essay was published, art had gone through a period of intense politicization, the high point of which was the 1993 Whitney Biennial, in which nearly every work was a shrill effort to change American society. Hickey's prediction did not precisely pan out. What happened was less the pursuit of beauty as such by artists than the pursuit of the idea of beauty, through a number of exhibitions and conferences, by critics and curators who, perhaps inspired by Hickey, thought it time to have another look at beauty.

A good example to consider is an exhibition that took place at the Hirschhorn Museum in Washington, in October 1999. In celebration of the museum's fiftieth anniversary, two curators—Neil Ben Ezra and Olga Viso—organized an exhibition called *Regarding Beauty: Perspectives on Art since 1950*. In 1996 the same two curators had mounted an apparently antithetical exhibition titled *Distemper: Dissonant Themes in the Art of the 1990s*. Only three years separate the two shows, but the contrast is sharp enough to have raised a question of whether there had not been some artistic turning point in this narrow interval—a hairpin turn in the *Kunstwollen*—and even a reappraisal of the social function of art. Dissonance had been the favored ambition for art for most of the preceding century. The shift from dissonance to beauty could hardly appear more extreme.

Olga Viso told me that it was the fact that many who saw the first show remarked to her on how beautiful many of the "dissonant" works struck them, that inspired her to put together a show just of art that was expressly made with beauty in mind. But if in fact the dissonance in contemporary art turned out to have been compatible with the works' being beautiful, dissonance could not have been quite so anti-aesthetic as the term and the spirit it expresses suggested. If, that is to say, the works from *Distemper* were found beautiful, they were probably not that different from the works in *Regarding Beauty* after all, and in fact that turned out to be the case. My own view, which will emerge more sharply as this book evolves, is that the beauty of the works in the earlier show would have been incidental rather than integral to their meaning, as was supposed to be the case in the second show. But still it would be there. By "integral" I will mean that the beauty is internal to the meaning of the work.

Consider, for illustrative purposes, the notorious example of Marcel Duchamp's perhaps too obsessively discussed *Fountain*, which, as by now everybody knows, largely consisted of an ordinary industrially produced urinal. Duchamp's supporters insisted that the urinal he anonymously submitted to the Society of Independent Artists in 1917 was meant to reveal how *lovely* this form really was—that abstracting from its function, the urinal looked enough like the exemplarily beautiful sculpture of Brancusi to suggest that Duchamp might have been interested in underscoring the affinities. It was Duchamp's patron, Walter Arensberg, who thought—or pretended to think—that disclosing the beauty was the point of *Fountain*—and Arensberg was a main patron of Brancusi as well.

Now Duchamp's urinal may indeed have been beautiful in point of form and surface and whiteness. But in my view, the beauty, if indeed there, was incidental to the work, which had other intentions altogether. Duchamp, particularly in his ready-mades of 1915–1917, intended to exemplify the most radical dis-

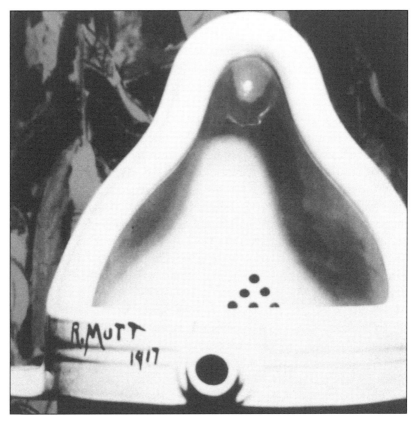

FIGURE 3 Marcel Duchamp, *Fountain*, 1917
The loveliness is incidental.

sociation of aesthetics from art. "A point which I very much want to establish is that the choice of these 'readymades' was never dictated by aesthetic delectation," he declared retrospectively in 1961. "The choice was based on a reaction of visual indifference with at the same time a total absence of good or bad taste . . . in fact a complete anesthesia." Still, Duchamp's supporters were aesthetically sensitive persons, and though they may have gotten his intentions wrong, they were not really mistaken about the fact, incidental or not, that the urinal really could be seen as beautiful. And Duchamp himself had said that modern plumbing was America's great contribution to civilization.

Let's say the supporters believed the beauty internal to the work, while I and many others think it incidental. But there can be no question that the work was, for many reasons, *dissonant*. So it could appear in an exhibition meant to thematize dissonance—or it could appear just as easily in a show called *Regarding Beauty*. And this might be quite generally the case, so that we can imagine two distinct exhibitions, but containing all and only the same works, the one show illustrating dissonance and the other illustrating beauty. The objects in both shows would in fact be beautiful, and in fact be dissonant. It might be unduly costly to put on two distinct shows, requiring two sets of largely indiscernible objects. One could instead simply have one show called *Distemper,* and then another called *Regarding Beauty,* and have them run one after the other by changing the banners outside the museum. Or we could have two entrances to the same show, those with a taste for dissonance entering through one and those with a thirst for beauty through the other. Mostly, I think, the two bodies of visitors would be satisfied with what they saw—though there would always be the danger of two people meeting inside, having split up since she has a taste for dissonance and he for beauty—and each then wondering if they had made a mistake, walking through the wrong entrance. All sorts of Shakespearean fun can be dreamed up. We could train the docents to say, to one set of visitors, that the beauty (or dissonance) was incidental in the one show and inherent in the other—but this is carrying things too far, since there are cases where beauty is internally related to the dissonance—where the work would not be dissonant if it were not beautiful. This would be the case with the two artists most closely associated with conservative attacks against the National Endowment of the Arts—Robert Mapplethorpe and Andres Serrano.

Readers will object that I am simply indulging my imagination, and letting it run wild. We all know that there are plenty of dissonant works that are not even incidentally beautiful, and plenty of beautiful works without any dissonant aspect at all. Can we not just work with clear-cut cases? The answer perhaps is No, and explaining why will be one of the merits of this book, if the explanation is sound. Meanwhile, it will be of some value to recognize that the connection between *Fountain* and the particular urinal that Duchamp appropriated is pretty close to that between Warhol's *Brillo Box* and the Brillo carton designed by James Harvey. It was the aesthetics of the latter that got me so interested in the former, which had no aesthetics to speak of, other than what it appropriated from Harvey's boxes. But then Harvey's boxes had none of the philosophical depth of Warhol's, for much the same reason that the urinal manufactured by Mott Iron Works had none of the philosophical—and artistic!—power of *Fountain*, which after all helped transform the history of art. But it would be questionable whether the aesthetic power of the urinals—which were designed to be attractive, the way the Brillo cartons were—belongs to *Fountain* as a work of art at all. For that matter, the dissonance of *Fountain* is not a property of urinals as such, which are perfectly straightforward fittings for bathrooms. In any case, there is a metaphysical question in distinguishing between *Fountain,* and the urinal it consisted of, not altogether different from distinguishing between a person and his or her body.

Born of the Spirit and Born Again

Since I am a philosopher with a known involvement with the artworld, I found myself invited to several of the conferences convened to discuss beauty, and I wrote a number of essays as well. The first time I had to confront the question of "Whatever Happened to Beauty?"—a conference sponsored by the Art History Department at the University of Texas in Austin in 1993—I found myself looking into Hegel's great work on aesthetics. Ever since I had begun to write on the subject of the End of Art, I found myself consulting Hegel, who of course had written on that same subject in the 1820s. His book became a kind of treasury of philosophical wisdom for me, in fact, and whenever I embarked on a subject new to me, I found it valuable to see if Hegel might not have had something to say about it. There were two thoughts, on the very first page of his work, which became deeply stimulating to me when I began to ponder the philosophy of beauty. One was the rather radical distinction he drew between natural and artistic beauty, in the very first lines of his text. And the other was his gloss on why artistic beauty seemed "superior" to natural beauty. It was because it was "born of the Spirit and born again." That was a grand ringing phrase: *Aus den Geistens geborene und wiedergeborene.* It meant, as I saw it, that artistic beauty was in some sense an intellectual rather than a natural product. That did not entail that the two kinds of beauty were, other than through their explanations, necessarily different. If someone painted a field of daffodils, to use a Romantic example, it might have been beautiful in just the same way a field of daffodils itself is beautiful. Still, the fact that the painting was "born of the spirit" meant that for Hegel it would have an importance that the natural phenomenon would lack. As always, I found profoundly stimulating the idea that two things might look quite alike but have very different meanings and identities—like *Brillo Box* and the Brillo boxes.

It was with this in my mind that I found a way of drawing a distinction that began to seem quite fruitful. I began to think that the beauty of an artwork could be internal to it, in the sense that it was part of the artwork's *meaning*. This idea dawned on me in thinking about Robert Motherwell's *Elegies for the Spanish Republic*, which I discuss at length in a later chapter of this book. Motherwell's paintings were, in some sense, political—after all they were occasioned by an event in the political history of Spain. Their patent beauty followed naturally from being elegies, since elegies are in their nature meant to be beautiful. Somehow the beauty of the elegy is intended to transform pain into something endurable. So the beauty would be internal to the meaning of the works. By contrast, the beauty of the urinal, if indeed urinals are beautiful, seemed to me quite external to *Fountain,* just as the aesthetics of the Brillo boxes were external to Warhol's *Brillo Box.* They were not part of the meaning. In truth I do not know what the aesthetics of Warhol's *Brillo Box,* if indeed it has any aesthetics, are. It, like *Fountain,* is essentially a conceptual work.

Motherwell, who was a close friend, had recently died, and though I am not a superstitious person, I could not help but feel that the distinction between internal and external beauty, and the connection of the two with meaning, was a sort of gift. I thought that what was distinctive of a work of art as against a natural phenomenon, was that it had some kind of meaning, which would go some distance toward rendering into somewhat contemporary terms Hegel's idea of something being born of the spirit and born again. The meaning of a work of art is an intellectual product, which is grasped through interpretation by someone other than the artist, and the beauty of the work, if indeed it is beautiful, is seen as entailed by that meaning. It was not difficult to find other examples. I thought, for example, of Maya Lin's *Vietnam Veterans' Memorial,* where the beauty is internally generated by the work's meaning. And many other examples were ready to hand. It was, in any case, the first time that I had found a piece of structure in the concept of beauty that might lend itself to philosophical analysis. It was perhaps not a lot of a structure—but it was something to begin to build a piece of philosophy with.

When I was invited to deliver the Carus Lectures before the American Philosophical Association at the annual meeting of its Eastern Division in 2001, I decided to devote them to the subject of beauty. It took a certain amount of nerve to stand up before that organization and talk about beauty—hardly any more a cutting-edge subject in philosophy than in art. But by that time I had found a way of connecting the history of modern art together with my own philosophical interest in the definition of art, and to put both together with the idea of internal as against external beauty. The present book develops the three Carus Lectures in a somewhat systematic way. It might be considered the third volume of a contemporary philosophy of art, the first being my 1981 *The Transfiguration of the Commonplace*, which works out what one might call the ontology of the artwork; and the second the 1997 *After the End of Art*, in which I develop what I think of as a philosophical history of art.

Initially, I felt somewhat sheepish about writing on beauty. This was a lingering consequence of the attitude toward aesthetics that prevailed in my early years in analytical philosophy—that the really serious work to be done by philosophy was in language and logic and the philosophy of science. I sometimes wondered if I ought not to be devoting the immense opportunity of the Carus Lectures to address some more mainstream philosophical topic—something closer to the collective heart of my profession. I had certain ideas, for example, on the concept of mental representation, which I would yet like to work out while I have the mind for it. But what had happened in art in the 1960s and afterward was a revolution, to the understanding of which my writings had somewhat contributed, and I felt that the passing from artistic consciousness of the idea of beauty was itself a crisis of sorts. But even if beauty proved far less central to the visual arts than had been taken for granted in the philosophical tradition, that did not entail that it was not central to human life. The spontaneous appearance of those moving improvised shrines everywhere in New York after the terrorist attack of September 11th, 2001, was evidence for me that the need for beauty in the extreme moments of life is deeply ingrained in the human framework. In any case I came to the view that in writing about beauty as a philosopher, I was addressing the deepest kind of issue there is. Beauty is but one of an immense range of aesthetic qualities, and philosophical aesthetics has been paralyzed by focusing as narrowly on beauty as it has. But beauty is the only one of the aesthetic qualities that is also a value, like truth and goodness. It is not simply among the values we live by, but one of the values that defines what a fully human life means.

Beauty and the Philosophical
Definition of Art

It is the mark of the present period in the history of art that the concept of art implies no internal constraint on what works of art are, so that one no longer can tell if something is a work of art or not. Worse, something can be a work of art but something quite like it not be one, since nothing that meets the eye reveals the difference. This does not mean that it is arbitrary whether something is a work of art, but only that traditional criteria no longer apply. The Whitney Biennial of 2002 included a performance piece by the collaborative *Praxis,* which offered visitors to its storefront space in New York's East Village choices from a menu of services, which included hugs, footbaths, dollar bills, and affixing band-aids accompanied by a kiss. One of Biennial 2002's most popular and moving works was a sound piece by Steven Vitiello, consisting of a 1999 recording of the sounds made by Hurricane Floyd outside the ninety-first floor of Tower One in the World Trade Center. Everything is now possible for visual artists, though one consequence of this radical openness is that being a work of art no longer exempts it from the sanctions it would be exposed to if it were just part of life. The would-be assassin of Andy Warhol,

Valerie Solanis, might convincingly have argued that she intended shooting him as a performance piece—but her First Amendment rights were uninfringed when she faced the legal consequences of attempted homicide. The composer Karlheinz Stockhausen proclaimed as "the greatest work of art ever" the terrorist attack on the World Trade Center in New York on September 11, 2001. As his language conveyed extreme admiration, he was instantly disgraced, but the fact that such a claim could be made at all underscores the total openness of the domain, however monstrous it would be to crash airliners into heavily occupied buildings in order to make a work of art.

"Anything" seems a thin and disillusioning answer to the question "What is art?" But that is because it was long assumed that works of art constituted a restricted and somewhat exalted set of objects that everyone would be able to identify as such, the question only being what accounted for their status. The mark of the contemporary condition in the *philosophy* of art is that a philosophical definition of art must be consistent with the radical openness that has overtaken the domain. It is still true that works of art constitute a restricted set of objects. What has changed is that these cannot easily be identified as such, since anything one can think of might be a work of art, and what accounts for this status cannot be a matter of simple recognition. It is by now well understood that something can resemble a work of art entirely and yet itself not be a work of art at all. This would hardly have seemed credible much before 1917, when Marcel Duchamp had already established an oeuvre of perhaps fourteen readymades. The set of readymades— a bicycle wheel, a snow-shovel, a plumbing fixture, a typewriter cover, a grooming comb for dogs, and the like—might far more resemble what might be found in a neighborhood garage sale than anything on display in the Louvre's *Salon Carré*. Duchamp, as we shall note, had somewhat severe criteria for which commonplace objects were in candidacy for the status of readymades, so even he might have wanted to draw a line that the subsequent evolution of the art world has more or less erased. And of course he left unaddressed the question of what entitled readymades to the status of artworks, while leaving unredeemed the objects in the garage sale. Or the latter from those in an as yet uncreated work of art— *Garage Sale*—which duplicates them exactly: a snow shovel, a typewriter cover, a plumbing fixture, and so forth.

In previous writings I have spoken of the present state of things as The End of Art—a characterization I imagine Adorno would have accepted, with the difference that he would do so as an expression of cultural despair, whereas I mean only that one can now begin seeking a philosophical definition of art without waiting to see what further, by way of objects, the future history of art will bring forth. Since anything can be a work of art, there may in the future be surprises, but they won't be philosophical surprises. A tenable philosophical definition of art will have to be compatible with whatever art there is. A critic once tried to remind me that a definition has to exclude something. But of course a philosophical definition of art covers all and only works of art. It excludes everything else. It excludes for example the hugs and kisses that the members of Praxis give when they are simply being affectionate, and not engaging in a piece of performance art. I salute Adorno for his astute recognition that, contrary to what philosophers traditionally believed about art, nothing, absolutely nothing, is any longer self-evident.

The posthumous publication of Adorno's book in 1969 coincided with the end of a decade of remarkably intense inquiry, conducted by artists as well as by philosophers, though largely in independence of one another. Or rather, the inquiry was entirely philosophical, though much of the philosophy and most of the best of it was produced by artists exploring the limits of art from within. A parallel between modernist art and a certain form of philosophical practice was remarked upon in an essay with which the decade properly began—Clement Greenberg's 1960 "Modernist Painting"—in which he compared modernism in art with a form of self-criticism exemplified in the philosophy of Kant, whom he complimented in consequence as the first modernist. Self-critique in the arts, as understood by Greenberg, consisted in purifying the medium unique to any art of whatever was extrinsic to it. In an example with which Greenberg's thought has been identified, *flatness* is what is unique to the medium of painting, which must accordingly be purged of illusionism of any kind, and depth given over by right to sculpture. Modernism had inherited much the same array of media that was available to artists at the time of Vasari, with the important if controverted exception of photography. In rendering itself "pure," Greenberg predicted, each art would "find the guarantee of its standards of quality as well as of its independence." But "respect for the medium" as a critical criterion too has vanished from contemporary discourse. Today anything goes with anything, in any way at all. Modernism, as Greenberg presented it, was a kind of conceptual cleansing, to borrow a scary political metaphor. In our post-modernist era, purity is an option, and pretty much out of fashion at that.

These issues notwithstanding, Greenberg's agenda was one of art defining itself from within, and there can be no question that this quasi-Kantian endeavor was pursued, often with a certain puritanical fervor, by a number of artists bent on making art in its conceptually purified condition. This was particularly the case with the so-called "Minimalists," and it is not difficult to see their program as parallel in many respect to philosophy as practiced by such figures as Nelson Goodman or indeed any philosophy based on a program of radical elimination or of reduction to some favored base—observation, behavior, or whatever. Whether there was an influence between such philosophies and artistic practice is difficult to say, but certain of the Minimalists studied at universities like Princeton and Columbia, where such philosophy was taught, and the minimalist slogan voiced by the painter, Frank Stella— "What you see is what you see"—expresses a not unfamiliar philosophical attitude of the time.

In truth, philosophy and avant-garde art in the 1960s shared a great many attitudes. One aim of Pop, for example, was to ironize the distinction between high and vernacular art—between the heroized painting of the previous generation of artists, the Abstract Expressionists, and the popular imagery of the comic strip and commercial advertisement—the "High and Low" of a controversial exhibition at the Museum of Modern Art in 1992. But comparably, it was an effort of analytical philosophy to overcome the pretensions of what we might call "high" philosophy—the cosmo-tragical visions of the Existentialists, or of the metaphysical titans who loomed behind them—by criticizing their language against either the standards of ordinary discourse, where we know whereof we speak, or of a scientific discourse governed by strict considerations of verifiability and confirmability. It is difficult to resist the impulse to see a cultural equivalence between canonization of ordinary language, cultivated by the Oxford School of Linguistic phenomenology, and the studied aesthetic of everyday objects in Warhol's Factory or Claes Oldenberg's 1962 Store on

East Second Street in Manhattan, where one could buy painted effigies of gym shoes, automobile tires, and women's underpants or tights. Philosophy was marked by a willed down-to-earthness in its examples. Wanting a sip of beer served as the paradigm of desire, turning the lights on or off by flipping a switch was (is) the standard example of human action.

Switching the lights on and off was tendered as a minimal work of art by the composer George Brecht, a member of Fluxus, a movement in which I have a particular interest, since my own philosophical ideas on art were first worked out in the early 1960s, when I knew nothing of Fluxus's thought or practice, though I now wish I had. It is perhaps one sign of a true movement of thought when individuals begin to do or think the same kinds of things while unaware of one another's existence, although there is a rather natural historical explanation for such parallels as may have existed between philosophical and artistic attitudes in the early sixties. The members of Fluxus were alumni of John Cage's seminar in experimental composition at the New School, and subscribed to certain ideas emanating from Dr. Suzuki's seminars in Zen Buddhism at Columbia, both of which took place in the late 1950s. Zen ideas, as framed by Suzuki, had a vast transformative influence on the intellectual life of New York in those years. My own thought, set out in the already mentioned 1964 article, "The Art World," is seasoned with imagery I acquired from sitting in on Suzuki's class, as well as from his books. Cage is widely known for his endeavor to overcome the distinction between music and mere noise—a program generalized by Fluxus as "closing the gap between art and life." In those crucial years, especially in and around New York, the commonplace world of everyday experience had begun to undergo a kind of transfiguration in artistic consciousness. And this is a direct consequence of Suzuki's teaching. I found it philosophically thrilling to realize that nothing outward need distinguish a work of art from the most ordinary of objects or events—that a dance can consist in nothing more remarkable than sitting still, that whatever one hears can be music—even silence. The plainest of wooden boxes, a coil of clothesline, a roll of chicken wire, a row of bricks, could be a sculpture. A simple shape painted white could be a painting. The institutions of high culture were not well suited to this moment. It was unreasonable to pay admission to watch a woman not move, or to listen to oneself breathe as someone else, sitting before a piano, did not touch the keys. So much the worse for the institutions of the art world! At any time the weather allowed, a group could assemble to perform Dick Higgins's 1959 *Winter Carol*, listening to the snow fall for an agreed upon period of time. What could be more magical? Anyone could perform Yoko Ono's early "instruction work," *Match Piece*, in which one strikes a match and watches it until the flame goes out. The dying of the light— what could be more poetic?

How much of any of this fell within the horizons of official aesthetics is historically problematic, but somehow the avant-garde, such as it was within that philosophical specialty, appeared to have understood that the definition of art had to be undertaken as if something like it were true. Richard Wollheim's "Minimal Art" appeared in 1965, initially in an art periodical, and Wollheim is credited with coining the term Minimalism, though he admits having known nothing of the works that finally became so designated. His concern, rather, was whether there are minimal criteria for something being art, and his paradigms were monochrome paintings, which existed only as philosophical jokes until perhaps 1915, and the ready-mades, which appeared in the history of art at more or less the same time. In this, Wollheim followed the official philosophical model according to which having a concept meant possessing criteria for picking out its instances. It was a Wittgensteinian commonplace that instances can be culled out successfully without benefit of definitions, as in the example that he made famous, of games. In fact there can be no criteria for distinguishing a ready-made metal grooming comb from an indiscernible metal grooming comb that was not a readymade, nor a monochrome white painting from a panel all over which white paint had been slathered—so the question of definition became urgent after all. The tried and true method of "picking out instances" loses its appeal when dealing with the inventory of Fluxus: George Brecht's 1975 *Valoche (A Flux Travel Aid)* is a wooden box containing toys: a jump rope, some balls, a top (perhaps), a children's block with a snowman painted on it, a chess piece, a plastic egg or two, and what might or might not be prizes from boxes of Crackerjack. Wittgenstein's prestige notwithstanding, his was probably always the wrong approach to such matters. He would not be the first philosophical genius whose central ideas and proposals were deeply wrong.

FIGURE 4   George Brecht, *Valoche (A Flux Travel Aid)*, 1975
Wittgenstein's approach won't work here.

My article, "The Art World," presented at the annual meeting of the American Philosophical Association in 1964, was based on the central difficulty that pairs of objects were now available, entirely alike so far as appearances went—*Valoche* or a mere box of toys—but such that one was a work of art and the other not. I first encountered this possibility earlier that year at an exhibition of Andy Warhol's cartons at the Stable Gallery in East 74th Street in Manhattan. His *Brillo Box* looked enough like the commercial cartons in which Brillo pads were packed that a photograph of one would look entirely like a photograph of the other. So what accounted for the difference? My sense at the time was that they would have different historical explanations—that Warhol's *Brillo Box*, for example, had been made by someone who had internalized the recent history of art and commanded a body of theory, for the benefit of those who also knew that history and those theories, by contrast with the actual Brillo carton of the supermarket, conceived of by a free-lance package designer, for those who had to decide how their product was to be shipped to supermarkets. Warhol's, by contrast, was made for an art world that was in position to appreciate it, which was George Dickie's formulation in his Institutional Theory of Art, according to which something is a work of art (a) if it is an artifact (b) upon which some person or persons acting on behalf of the art world has conferred the wary status of a "candidate for appreciation." In art-historical fact, there was no *the* Art World in the 1960s, but a number of overlapping groups of artists and critics, many of whom were prepared to say that what others were doing was not really art at all. In 1963, Richard Artschwager sent a dozen identical kits to various institutions and individuals he thought might be interested in his work. The Guggenheim Museum responded that it was craft, not art. The director of the Castelli Gallery invited him to come round. What gives any art world its authority can hardly be answered without a more cognitivist definition than Dickie's, but I'll not pursue the matter here.

Philosophers like to appeal to "our" concept of this or that. Wollheim worried that a certain artistic practice would result in "the disintegration of our concept of 'art' as we have it." But in truth very little of "our" concept actually survived the avant-garde experiments of the sixties. What was revolutionary about Fluxus was that it removed from the received conception of art almost everything that had been thought to ground the distinction, as in the following partial catalog I excerpt from George Maciunas's 1966 *Fluxus Manifesto*: "Exclusiveness, Individuality, Ambition . . . Significance, Rarity, Inspiration, Skill, Complexity, Profundity, Greatness, Institutional and Commodity Value." Here in the same spirit is an agenda articulated by Yvonne Rainer in an agenda for the Judson Dance Group: "NO to spectacle no to virtuosity no to transformations and magic and make believe no to the glamour and transcendency of the star image." With the advent of Conceptual art at the end of the decade, it was no longer required that there be a material object (an "artifact"?), nor was it necessary that, if there were in fact an object, it had to be made by the artist. One could make the art without being an artist, or be an artist without making the art for which one claimed credit. "I've stopped making objects," the artist Douglas Huebner said in a 1969 interview. "And I'm not trying to take anything away from the world. Nor am I trying to restructure the world. I'm not trying to tell the world anything, really. I'm not trying to tell the world that it could be better by being this or that. I'm just, you know, touching the world by doing these things, and leaving it pretty much the way it is." Leaving the world as we found it, we had been told by Wittgenstein, this time profoundly, is the way it is with philosophy. Artists need not follow in the footsteps of Huebner, but at least they can and still be artists. The definition of art would have to be built on the ruins of what had been thought to be the concept of art in previous discourses.

Beauty Dethroned

What follows from this history of conceptual erasure is not that art is indefinable, but that the conditions necessary for something to be art will have to be fairly general and abstract to fit all imaginable cases, and in particular that very little remains of "our concept of art" that the framer of a real definition can rely on. In *The Transfiguration of the Commonplace* I advanced two conditions, condensed as "x is an art work if it embodies a meaning," the chief merit of which lay in its weakness. Missing from my proto-definition, as from all the definitions of the sixties known to me, was any reference to beauty, which would surely have been among the first conditions to have been advanced by a conceptual analyst at the turn of the twentieth century. Beauty had disappeared not only from the advanced art of the 1960s, but from the advanced philosophy of art of that decade as well. Nor *could* it really be part of the definition of art if anything can be an artwork, when not everything is beautiful. Beauty might be listed as a disjunct in the vocabulary of appreciation, and hence covered by Dickie's main concept. But beauty rarely came up in art periodicals from the 1960s on without a deconstructionist snicker. Not long after the John Simon

Guggenheim Memorial Foundation was established in 1925, the founders saw as its immediate beneficiaries "Men and women devoted to pushing the forward the boundaries of knowledge and to the creation of beauty." Art was tacitly defined in terms of creating beauty, and creating beauty is put on equal footing with expanding the boundaries of knowledge. The logo of the Institute for Advanced Studies in Princeton in 1930 shows two allegorical females, one draped and the other nude, labeled Beauty and Truth in that order, the garment perhaps implying that Beauty is Truth with a dress on. But reference to the creation of beauty all but drops out of the enabling language for the National Endowment for the Arts, about forty years later, not just because beauty had largely disappeared from the artistic agenda in 1965, but because, we learn from Michael Brenson's recent study of the NEA, its sponsors saw artists as sources of ideas which might be of value in the national agenda of winning the Cold War.

In those years, nevertheless, modern art was dismissed as subversive and destructive, and essentially anti-American by such figures as Congressman George A. Dondero of Michigan, who wrote "Modern art is communistic because it is distorted and ugly, because it does not glorify our beautiful country, our cheerful and smiling people, and our material progress. Art which does not beautify our country in plain simple terms that everyone can understand breeds dissatisfaction. It is therefore opposed to our government and those who create and promote it are our enemies." The newspaper magnate William Randolph Hearst, Brenson states, "equated any form of artistic radicalism with communism, and assumed that of the work produced in a non-traditional manner was a disguised means of communist propaganda." This is but one instance, as we shall see, of the politicization of beauty.

In the early 1990s, the critic Dave Hickey was asked what he thought the central issue of the decade would be. "Snatched from my reverie, I said 'Beauty,' and then, more firmly, 'The issue of the nineties will be *beauty.*'" This was greeted, he recalls, with a "total uncomprehending silence . . . I had wandered into this *dead zone,* this silent abyss." Let me begin to put this the silence into one possible perspective by considering the photography of Robert Mapplethorpe, which had become notorious in 1989 when his exhibition, *The Perfect Moment,* was cancelled by the Corcoran

Museum of Art in an ill-advised pre-emptive move against the danger that funding for the National Endowment of the Arts might be voted down if our legislators saw what the fund was supporting. The fear was based on the charged sexual content of his signature images—though it was central to Mapplethorpe's achievement that his work was self-consciously beautiful as well. It was its beauty, rather than its often gamy content, that alienated the photographic avant-garde from him as an artist. When I was writing my book on Mapplethorpe, *Playing with the Edge,* I asked a photographer who was at the time experimenting with pinhole cameras what he thought of him. He dismissed Mapplethorpe as a *pompier*—an artist so concerned with elegance as to have lost touch with the limits of his medium. The imperatives of Modernism tended to make the simple grainy snapshot the paradigm of photographic purity, which applies to photography Greenberg's purgative view of the quest for what is inherent in the medium. The charge against Mapplethorpe was that his work was too beautiful to qualify for critical endorsement. "One writer claimed that if I painted sex and violence, it would have been okay, but one isn't allowed to paint anything beautiful," Gerhard Richter recalls. "The changed fashion of the time," if I may appropriate Kant's mournful language regarding the fate of Metaphysics, "brings beauty only scorn; a matron outcast and forsaken."

There is more to the dethronement of beauty, however, than the discovery that it has no place in the definition of a given art, or, in the light of post-modernist pluralism, in the definition of art in general. There is the widespread sense that in some way beauty trivializes that which possesses it. The casual philosophy of beauty has rested content with the thought, often ascribed to David Hume, that it is merely in the eye of the beholder. Hume indeed held, in the essay *Of Civil Liberty,* "that beauty in things exists in the mind"—but this in no sense distinguished it, for Hume, from anything else, inasmuch as "tastes and colours, and all other sensible qualities, lie not in bodies but in the senses,"as he writes in "The Skeptic."

> The case is the same with beauty and deformity, virtue and vice. This doctrine, however takes off no more from the reality of the latter qualities than from that of the former . . . Though colours were allowed to lie only in the eye, would dyers or painters ever be less regarded or esteemed? There is a sufficient uniformity in the senses

ıd feelings of mankind to make all these qualities the objects of art ınd reasoning, and to have the greatest influence on life and manners.

But even a philosophical argument that beauty might claim the same ontological weight as virtue and vice would not entirely erase the felt sense that there is something almost derelict or even indecent in the pursuit of beauty—an attitude that does not arise with the other aesthetic categories we were advised by Oxford analysts to canvas if we were interested in making some progress in aesthetics—"the dainty and the dumpy," to cite J.L. Austin's examples. But none of them carries the moral weight of beauty in the aesthetic tradition. The real conceptual revolution, in truth, is not purging the concept of art of aesthetic qualities so much as purging the concept of beauty of the moral authority one feels it must have possessed in order that possessing beauty should have come to be taken as morally questionable. At the height of the Vietnam War, the painter Philip Guston bade farewell to the beautiful paintings on which his reputation was based, and instead began to paint allegories of evil that could not consistently with their intended moral message possess the stigma of beauty.

In a letter to Thomas Monro in 1927, George Santayana wrote of his generation "We were not very much later than Ruskin, Pater, Swinburne, and Matthew Arnold. Our atmosphere was that of poets and persons touched with religious enthusiasm or religious sadness. Beauty (which mustn't be mentioned now) was then a living presence, or an aching absence, day and night." It was precisely its beauty that justified the esteem in which art was held in Santayana's time. Here, for example, are some thoughts from the early writing of Santayana's contemporary, G.E. Moore, that are almost unintelligible today: "I cannot see but what that which is meant by beautiful is simply and solely that which is an end in itself. The object of art would then be that to which the objects of Morals are means, and the only thing to which they are means. The only reason for having virtues would be to produce works of art." In his early text, *Art, Morals, and Religion,* Moore wrote: "Religion is merely a subdivision of art," which he explicated this way: "Every valuable purpose which religion serves is also served by Art; and Art perhaps serves more if we are to say that its range of good objects and emotions is wider." There can be no doubt that Moore believed that art can take religion's purposes over because of the beauty it essentially possesses. Proust was greatly moved by the 1897 work by Robert de Sizeranne titled *Ruskin et la religion de la beauté*.

Now I would like to offer an historical speculation. It is that the immense esteem in which art continues to be held today is an inheritance of this exalted view of beauty. It is widely and some-times cynically said that art has replaced religion in contemporary consciousness. My speculation is that these Victorian or Edwardian attitudes have survived the abjuration of beauty itself. I will go even further and suggest that if there is a place for beauty in art today, it is connected with these survivals, which are deeply embedded in human consciousness. Beauty's place is not in the definition or, to use the somewhat discredited idiom, the essence of art, from which the avant-garde has rightly removed it. That removal, however, was not merely the result of a conceptual but, as I shall argue, a political determination. And it is the residue of aesthetic politics that lingers on in the negativity we find in atti-tudes toward beauty in art today. The idea of beauty, the poet Bill Berkson wrote me recently, is a "mangled sodden thing." But the *fact* of beauty is quite another matter. In a passage near the begin-ning of *Within a Budding Grove,* Marcel (the Narrator), traveling by train to Balbec, sees a peasant girl approaching the station in the early morning, offering coffee and milk. "I felt on seeing her that desire to live which is reborn in us whenever we become conscious anew of beauty and of happiness." I believe Proust's psychology profound in connecting the consciousness of beauty with the feel-ing of happiness—which has also been trivialized in modernist times—providing we are not conflicted because of a negativity that had not inflected the idea of beauty in the generation of Proust, Moore, and Santayana. I would like to press this further. It was the moral weight that was assigned to beauty that helps us understand why the first generation of the avant-garde found it so urgent to dislodge beauty from its mistaken place in the philosophy of art. It occupied that place in virtue of a conceptual error. Once we are in position to perceive that mistake, we should be able to redeem beauty for artistic use once again. Conceptual analysis, without the reinforcement of a kind of Foucauldian archeology, is insufficiently powerful to help us in this task. Had it not, for example, been for the artistic avant-garde in the twentieth century, philosophers almost certainly would continue to teach that the connection between art and beauty is conceptually tight. It took the energy of the artistic avant-garde to open a rift between art and beauty that would previously have been unthinkable—that, as we shall see, remained unthinkable long after it was opened, largely because the connection between art and beauty was taken to have the power of an a priori necessity.

Moore's Revelation

In the latter sections of *Principia Ethica,* Moore wrote "By far the most valuable things we know or can imagine, are certain states of consciousness, which may roughly be described as the pleasures of human intercourse and the enjoyment of beautiful objects." He thought the point "so obvious that it risks seeming to be a platitude." No one, Moore claims, "has ever doubted that personal affection and the appreciation of what is beautiful in Art or Nature, are good in themselves." Nor, he continues, "does it appear probable that any one will think that anything else has *nearly* so great a value as the things which are included under these two heads." Moore's confident appeals seem today almost shockingly parochial, but I'll suppose they were commonplace in his world. What would not have been commonplace, however, is what he next goes on to claim, namely that "this is the ultimate and fundamental truth of Moral Philosophy" and that these two values "form the rational ultimate end of human action and the sole criterion of social progress." People might come to accept these as truths, but they appear, Moore said, to be "truths which have been generally overlooked."

I think Moore must have been correct that if these were truths, they were generally overlooked, since they were received as having the force of revelation by the Bloomsbury circle, whose entire philosophy of art and of life derived from Moore's teaching and his example. In *My Early Beliefs,* John Maynard Keynes characterized Moore's ideas as "Exciting, exhilarating, the beginning of a renaissance, the opening of a new heaven on a new earth, we were the forerunners of a new dispensation, we were not afraid of anything . . . one's prime objects in life were love, the creation and enjoyment of aesthetic experience and the pursuit of knowledge. "A great new freedom seemed about to come," according to Vanessa Bell. When Lady Ottoline Morrell died in 1938, she was memorialized with a surprisingly uninspired epitaph, considering the literary stature of its authors—T.S. Eliot and Virginia Woolf: "a brave spirit, unbroken,/Delighting in beauty and goodness/And the love of her friends." Any member of the Bloomsbury circle, to which Woolf and Lady Ottoline centrally and Eliot marginally belonged, would wish to have been memorialized in precisely these terms. Puccini's librettist for *Tosca* put what in effect were Bloombury ideals in the heroine's aria: *Vissi d'arte, vissi d'amore*— I lived for art, I lived for love." The opera was staged in 1900— *Principia Ethica* was published in 1903—though set in the year 1800, when it seems to me a person like Tosca would have said that she had lived for *pleasure*, which was the central concept in Enlightenment moral psychology, as we can see even in Kant, when he addresses the topic of beauty. I find it hard to believe anyone lived for art in 1800, though this would have been the romanticist's philosophy of life. But love and art—and art because of its beauty—were precisely the defining values of Bloomsbury, whose scheme of values derived from *Principia Ethica*. Love and friendship, on the one hand, and what Moore speaks of "as the proper appreciation of a beautiful object" were to suffice, without the need for religion, the main moral needs of modern human beings.

Beauty Is Universal

With the exceptions of Hume and Hegel, the classical aestheticians drew no crucial distinction between "Art or Nature" in regard to the appreciation of beauty, and it must be borne in mind that that indifference was but rarely contested in philosophical aesthetics or in artistic practice itself when Moore composed *Principia Ethica*. If anything, I think, Moore supposed the appreciation of natural beauty superior to the appreciation of artistic beauty, largely because "We do think that the emotional contemplation of a natural scene, supposing its qualities equally beautiful, is in some way a better state of things than that of a painted landscape; we would think that the world would be improved if we could substitute for the best works of representative art *real* objects equally beautiful."

This merits an aside. At one point Moore invites us to consider two worlds. "Imagine the first "as beautiful as you can; put into it whatever on this earth you most admire—mountains, rivers, the sea; trees and sunsets, stars and moon." Imagine the other as "simply one heap of filth, containing everything that is most disgusting to us . . . and the whole, as far as may be, without one redeeming feature." Now "the only thing we are not entitled to imagine is that any human being ever has or ever, by any possibility, *can* ever see and enjoy the beauty of the one or hate the foulness of the other." Moore's argument now takes on logical energy on which the Ontological Argument turns, and we may paraphrase him in its terms. These two worlds now have, since we have imagined them, what earlier philosophers would have designated "objective reality." That is, they have the reality of something we have succeeded in thinking about—they are "objects of thought." Would it not be intrinsically better that they have—using again the earlier philosophical idiom—*formal* reality as well? Would it not be better, that is, that the beautiful rather than the ugly world actually exist, though no one can enjoy it? "The instance is extreme," Moore concedes. And he concedes as well "that our beautiful world would be better still, if there were human beings in it to contemplate and enjoy its beauty." This of course is what Moore is really interested in, though it remains important to him that "the beautiful world *in itself* is better than the ugly."

I happen to believe that Moore's characteristically ingenious argument has a great deal of psychological truth. I mean that there are descriptions of states of affairs that would be accepted as beautiful and as ugly pretty much by anyone, especially in contrast to one another. As an example of the first, here is an observation by the art critic and moralist, John Berger:

> In Istanbul, the domestic interior, in both the shantytowns and elsewhere, is a place of repose, in profound opposition to what lies outside the door. Cramped, badly roofed, crooked, cherished, these interiors are spaces like prayers, both because they oppose the traffic of the world as it is, and because they are a metaphor for the garden of Eden or Paradise.
>
> Interiors symbolically offer the same things as Paradise: repose, flowers, fruit, quiet, soft materials, sweetmeats, cleanliness, femininity. The offer can be as imposing (and vulgar) as one of the Sultan's rooms in the harem, or it can be as modest as the printed pattern on a square of cheap cotton, draped over a cushion on the floor of a shack.

With variations in taste and circumstance, such symbolic Edens—interiors or gardens—would incorporate more or less the kinds of things and qualities Berger enumerates. I have encountered a contrastingly stark description by a Central American guerilla, of how to treat prisoners whose will and spirit one wants to break: shut them up in cold damp spaces without light of any sort, with vermin and bad food, surrounded by their own excrement. It is what one might term aesthetic torture. Choosing which of these conditions is preferable is not a matter of *taste*! Offered the choice, everyone would choose Paradise over jungle hell. Beauty may indeed be subjective, but it is universal, as Kant insisted. And this must be the intuition that underlies Moore's thought that connects beauty with goodness and connects beauty and happiness for Proust. It connects with something inherent in human nature, which would explain why aesthetic reality is as important as it is, and why aesthetic deprivation—depriving individuals of beauty—should have taken on the importance it did in the artistic agendas of the avant-garde.

Good Art May Not Be Beautiful

In any case, Moore believed that so far as the pictorial arts are concerned, a beautiful painting is a painting of a beautiful subject. And this I think gave a certain importance to the museum of fine arts which began to be seen as a site in which to experience beauty in those years. In Henry James's novel, *The Golden Bowl* (1905), his character, Adam Verver, a man of immense wealth living abroad, has conceived the idea of building a "museum of museums" for "American City," which gave him his wealth. He is doing this to "release the people of his native state from the bondage of ugliness." There would be no way—or no easy way—to transform Detroit or Pittsburgh into the Catskills or the Grand Canyon. But artistic beauty was portable, and if the aesthetically deprived citizenry of American City could be put in the presence of "treasures sifted to positive sanctity," this would be an immense benefit if Moore were right that contemplation of beautiful objects is of the highest moral good. It helps explain why museum architectures should have taken the form of the temple in James's time.

The problem was that Modernist painting at just that moment was beginning to veer, somewhat starkly, away from the mimetic model. Roger Fry, Moore's disciple, was a modernist painter and critic. He organized two notorious "Post Impressionist" exhibitions at the Grafton Gallery in London, in 1910 and in 1912, in which artistic representations so deviated from the motifs they transcribed, that even professional art critics saw no way of dealing with them. Fry wrote: "The generality of critics have given vent to their dislike and contempt in unequivocal terms. One gentleman is so put to it to account for his own inability to understand these pictures that he is driven to the conclusion that it is a colossal hoax on the part of the organizers of the exhibition and myself in particular." Here is Fry's attempt to explain their incapacity to see what the Bloomsbury Moderns and, for that matter, Moore himself, who came to think of the 1910 exhibition as the most important event of that year, regarded as the objective beauty in these unprecedented works:

> Almost without exception, they tacitly assume that the aim of art is imitative representation, yet none of them has tried to show any reason for such a curious proposition. A great deal has been said about these artists searching for the ugly instead of consoling us with beauty. They forget that *every new work of creative design is ugly until it becomes beautiful*; that we usually apply the word beautiful to those works of art in which familiarity has enabled us to grasp the unity easily, and that we find ugly those works in which we still perceive only by an effort. (Italics mine)

The perception of them as ugly is in effect, on Fry's view, the projection onto them of a mental confusion, which a course of aesthetic education will remove, enabling their beauty to be seen. Post-Impressionist painters, Fry goes on to say, affirm "the paramount importance of design, which necessarily places the imitative side of art in a secondary place." This is the basis of Fry's formalism.

But Fry himself made a mistake even more profound than thinking it the aim of painting to imitate nature. The mistake is that it is the aim of paintings to be beautiful. I give Fry great credit for thinking that something needed to be explained in order that those who scoffed might perceive the excellence of Post-Impressionist painting, just as Bloomsbury did, but I draw special attention to the a priori view that the painting in question really *was* beautiful, if only viewers knew how to look at it. It is a commonplace that the history of modernism is the history of acceptance. This story is told over and over by docents and lecturers in art appreciation. The history of art always has a happy ending.

Manet's *Olympia,* vilified in 1865, was a world treasure a century later, and that supports a little homily on critical restraint. In *The Guermantes Way,* Proust writes of the way "the unbridgeable gulf between what they considered a masterpiece by Ingres and what they supposed must for ever remain a 'horror' (Manet's *Olympia,* for example) shrink until the two canvases seemed like twins." How does this happen? Fry believed that it happens through critical explanation. People have to be brought to understand the work, and then they will see the way in which it is excellent. That, more than the actual explanations Fry gave, is his great achievement. For it makes clear that artistic goodness often requires explanation if it is to be appreciated, something that Hume understood completely. "In many orders of beauty, particularly those of the finer arts," Hume writes in Section One of his *Enquiry Concerning the Principles of Morals,* "it is requisite to employ much reasoning in order to feel the proper sentiment; and a false relish may frequently be corrected by argument and reflection." Hume is eager to point out that "moral beauty partakes much of this latter species."

With qualification, I accept Fry's point, as well as the spirit of Hume's marvelous observation. What I want to deny, however, is that the history of appreciation always culminates in the appreciation of *beauty.* It may indeed culminate in the appreciation of artistic goodness, which is what Hume really wanted to argue for in his great essay on how critically—and objectively—to arbitrate differences in taste. The mistake was to believe that artistic goodness is identical with beauty and that the perception of artistic goodness is the aesthetic perception of beauty. But that, as I see it, was the assumption of Edwardian Aesthetics, which the kind of art selected for the Grafton Gallery exhibitions ought to have called into question. The Edwardians, for example, were entirely right to begin to appreciate African art. They were even right in thinking that, on formal grounds, it could be seen as beautiful. The Victorians had thought that "primitive peoples" were, in making art, trying to make beautiful objects, only they did not know exactly how— hence their "primitivity." The Edwardians thought themselves advanced because formalism enabled them to see what Fry called "Negro sculpture" as beautiful. But they were wrong in thinking that they had learned through formalism to see the beauty that was the point of African art. That was never its point, nor was beauty the point of most of the world's great art. It is very rarely the point of art today.

Having lived through the *Sensation* exhibition at the Brooklyn Museum in 1999, we can sympathize with Fry. The critics pretty much to a person condemned the art, and were certain they were being put upon. But they were ready to see it as a First Amendment rather than an aesthetic matter, and in this they were perhaps more right than someone would have been who hoped that through argument one would at last see the beauty. It is not and it never was the destiny of all art ultimately to be seen as beautiful. There would have been no way for David Hume to have known about this, And it was perhaps historically too early for Roger Fry to have known about it as well, not least of all because the art that was so difficult for his contemporaries to accept often turned out to be artistically good in just the way he anticipated and Hume explained—through patient critical analysis. A lot of what prevented people from seeing the excellence of early modern paintings were inapplicable theories of what art should be. But that did not mean that even when one came around to see that the art that had so alarmed and enraged Fry's critics was after all good, one was going to see it as beautiful! Matisse's *Blue Nude* is a good,

FIGURE 5   Henri Matisse, *Blue Nude*, 1907
Possibly great, definitely unbeautiful

even a great painting—but someone who claims it is beautiful is talking through his or her hat. In order to find in what way beauty can have a role to play in the art of our time, we shall have to free ourselves from the Edwardian axiom that good art is categorically beautiful, if only we recognized how. It is an achievement of the conceptual history of art in the twentieth century that we have a very much more complex idea of artistic appreciation than was available to the early Modernists—or to Modernism in general, down to its formulation in the writing of Clement Greenberg as late as the 1960s. I'll take this up in the next chapter, which addresses what I designate as the Intractable Avant-Garde.

2

The Intractable Avant-Garde

I have a mad and starry desire to assassinate beauty . . .

TRISTAN TZARA

Near the opening of *A Season in Hell*—allegedly an allegorical account of his tumultuous relationship with the poet Paul Verlaine—Rimbaud writes: "One evening, I sat Beauty on my knees; and I found her bitter, and I abused her." The "bitterness of beauty" became epidemic among the avant-garde artists of the following century, but it was a rare thought in 1873 when Rimbaud published this poem. In Fantin-Latour's group portrait of the previous year, *Un Coin de Table*, Rimbaud is shown seated with Verlaine and a number of other bohemians in a group called *Les villains bonhommes—The Bad Eggs*—of whom Verlaine and Rimbaud were one might say the "baddest." The portrait of Rimbaud—the only true likeness of him we possess—is of a singularly beautiful, almost angelic-looking youth with golden curls, shown in a pensive state. He was eighteen and a rakehell; and the disparity between his character and his appearance, as in Oscar Wilde's character, Dorian Gray, is a familiar failure of fit that has helped give beauty a bad name. His badness extends even to his aesthetic preferences, which he catalogs in the *Délires* section of his poem: "Idiotic pictures, shop signs, stage sets, backcloths for street-entertainers, billboards, vernacular images, old fashioned stories, church Latin, badly spelt pornography, romance novels for elderly ladies, fairy tales, little books for children, old operas, silly

refrains, naïve rhythms." What Rimbaud would not have known
was that his inventory was to fit the canon of an alternative aesthetic a century later, under the name of "camp."

Though I have no wish to lose myself in interpreting
Rimbaud's poem, it can, perhaps must be read as a tribute to the
power of beauty, the disparities notwithstanding. Until he abused
Beauty in the third line, his life had been a celebration, "in which
every heart was opened and wine flowed freely." But now it is as if
the poet were sentenced to madness—a season in hell—in penalty.
He explicitly titles the section of the poem in which he declares his
anti-aesthetic preferences as *Ravings.* That section ends with what
feels like Rimbaud coming to his senses, though it can be read as
heavy irony: "All that's behind me now. Today I know how to bow
down before beauty." It is as if Rimbaud intuited a thought I can
hardly suppose he could have read in Kant's *Critique of Judgment,*
that "the beautiful is the symbol of the morally good."

Kant's text is not entirely easy to follow, but he clearly wants to
say that finding something beautiful is more than simply taking
pleasure in experiencing it. The beautiful "gives pleasure with a
claim for the agreement of everyone else." For this reason, "the
mind is made conscious of a certain ennoblement and elevation
above the mere sensibility of pleasure received through sense, and
the worth of others is estimated in accordance with a like maxim
of their judgment." In enunciating recently the principles of décor
that had been followed in creating a home for former prison
inmates, the director said "We tried to do this beautiful because
beautiful matters. Beautiful tells people they matter." Kant goes on
to claim "the subjective principle in judging the beautiful is represented as *universal,* i.e., valid for every man." The abuse of beauty,
on this view, is the symbolic enactment of an offense against morality and hence in effect against humanity. "I had armed myself
against justice," Rimbaud says just after confessing his crime, the
poem describing the price he paid.

Anthropology of Beauty

It is not clear, even if it would have been possible for him to have
imagined it, that the abuse of beauty would be regarded by Kant
as *ipso facto* a moral evil, since beauty only *symbolizes* morality, and
between moral and aesthetic judgments there is only the kind of

analogy, to use his example, that may hold between a common-wealth and a living body. So aesthetic imperatives are moral imperatives only symbolically. Kant recognizes that not everyone will agree, case by case, on questions of beauty, but the analogy requires the belief that they ought to, whatever may be the force of the ought. There was an Enlightenment tendency to believe that the same moral principles—the Golden Rule for example—were to be found in every society, so universality must have seemed co-extensive with humanity. Would there have been a parallel view in regard to beauty? Kant interestingly handled moral and aesthetic differences in systematically parallel ways. He learned about the South Seas from reading Captain Cook's voyages, and clearly he was struck by the otherness of the societies Cook describes. The question comes up for him whether those other lives are ones *we* would morally be able to live. In the schedule of cases in which he attempts to illustrate the working of the categorical imperative, he considers a talented individual in comfortable circumstances who "prefers indulgence in pleasure to troubling himself with broadening and improving his fortunate natural gifts." It would be entirely consistent with the laws of nature that everyone should live like "the inhabitants of the South Seas," so by one formulation of the categorical imperative, it would be permissible that a man "should let his talents rust and resolve to dedicate his life only to idleness, indulgence, and propagation" (Kant cannot bring himself to think of sex, even in the South Seas, in terms other than those of generation!) But *we* "cannot possibly will that this should become a universal law of nature, for "as a rational being, one necessarily wills that all one's faculties should be developed inasmuch as they are given to one for all sorts of possible purposes." The implication is that the South Sea islanders are not quite rational, but even so ought to live in conformity with the Protestant ethic, and that is what we must teach them as moral missionaries. Kant was in no sense a moral relativist. What relativists regard as differences in culture Kant will regard as but differences in development on the model of the differences between children and adults. The South Sea islanders are primitive Europeans, as a child is a primitive adult.

But Kant similarly contests South Sea aesthetics, as he understands them. Presumably based on anthropological illustrations he must have seen, Kant was aware that there are parts of the world in which men are covered with a kind of spiral tattoo: "We could adorn a figure with all kinds of spirals and light but regular lines, as the New Zealanders do with their tattooing, if only it were not the figure of a human being," he writes in the *Critique of Judgment*; and in the same section of that book he says "We could add much to a building, which would immediately please the eye if only it were not to be a church." These are imperatives of taste, and it is striking that Kant considers the tattoo as merely a form of ornamentation, say like gilded statuary on a church, rather than a set of marks which may, in anthropological truth, have nothing to

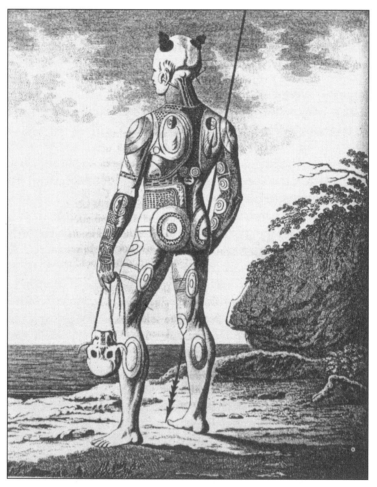

FIGURE 6 Engraving of a tattooed man
Something other than ornamentation

do with beautification, but serve rather to connect the tattooed person with some larger scheme of the world. The tattoo may conduce to admiration of its bearer—but not for aesthetic reasons so much as for whatever it is in a person the tattoo signified—military prowess, say, or cosmic rank, or as evidence of having come through some ordeal. Similarly with the brass neck coils affected by the Paduang women of Burma. The number and height of the coils may imply that the wearer is a figure of substance without this implying that it is an attribute of beauty. And something of the same sort may be true of ornament in, say, the German baroque church Kant evidently finds offensive to taste—as if the passions of Northern European Iconoclasm were merely expressions of aesthetic revulsion. It is, then, with reference to cognitive rather than aesthetic judgments that both ought to be assessed. I would hesitate to say that all cases of so-called beautification can be deflected in this way, but the possibility suggests that a universal beauty may be entirely consistent with cultural differences, our mistake consisting in regarding certain things as aesthetic when they have some quite different and more cognitive function. The aesthetic diversity of the world's art is consistent with beauty as such being everywhere more or less the same, if one cared to defend that thesis, and that wherever it were found it would evoke the same sense of ennoblement in its beholders.

If, on the other hand, tattooing in the South Seas really is beautiful "in the eye of the South Sea Islander," Kant must feel himself entitled to the view that they are just wrong. They just don't know what beauty is, which he would have defined in terms of what we may as well term the Protestant Aesthetic. Even Hegel, the first major philosopher I know of who actually went out of his way to look at paintings and listen to music, and was as we shall see an extraordinary art critic, had a difficult time with other traditions. "The Chinese," he states in his *Lectures on the Philosophy of History*, "have as a general characteristic, a remarkable skill in imitation, which is exercised not merely in daily life but in art. They have not yet succeeded in representing the beautiful as beautiful; for in their painting, perspective and shadow are wanting." Parenthetically, Clement Greenberg noted at one point that Manet pushed shadows to the edges of his forms—the way, Greenberg surmises, that he saw them in photographs—and this inevitably flattened his figures, which accounts in some measure for the outcry against his work, and at the same time explains how Greenberg should have regarded Manet as the first modernist painter, having stumbled onto the flatness that Greenberg declared the defining attribute of painting. Hegel's implication in any case is that the Chinese have either no idea of beauty or a wrong one. Unlike the artists of Oceania or Africa, they really do draw in ways that imply mimetic competence. The Chinese "observes accurately how many scales a carp has; how many indentations there are in the leaves of a tree, etc. [but] the Exalted, the Ideal and beautiful is not the domain of his art and skill." It would obviously sound crazy to characterize a great civilization like China's as primitive. In fact it was somewhat crazy to think of the Oceanic or African artists as primitive, with the assumption that they were trying to achieve beauty through accurate mimesis, but were, like children, not up to the task, and simply needed a robust *beaux arts* education. Hegel notes, sourly, that the Chinese are "too proud to learn anything from Europeans, although they must often recognize their [our] superiority." In historical fact, the Chinese did recognize the objective correctness of western perspective when they were shown it by missionaries in the seventeenth century. Their attitude was in effect "So what?"—not that there is no such thing as correct and incorrect, but that optical correctness had no bearing on painting as they practiced it in their culture. Chinese art in any case was beautiful enough to have been appropriated for decorative purposes in Europe from the seventeenth century on. But the Chinese culture had a very different idea of the aims of representation and of the relevance of visual truth. Yet no one could count their art as ugly, which is the operative thought in Roger Fry's dictum that things will be perceived as ugly until they are perceived as beautiful. It was Hegel who required aesthetic education, fixated as he was on the renaissance paradigm of mimesis as the ideal. But like everyone, as he says in his Preface to *The Philosophy of Right*, he was a child of his times.

Roger Fry understood, as a modernist, that the ligature between beauty and mimetic representation had been irreversibly loosened in his time. He knew that one could not argue the hostile reviewers of his exhibition into agreeing that Cézanne or Picasso show the world as we really see it—though there were certainly theorists prepared to argue that they had. Fry had instead to argue that this is not relevant, and that the emphasis must be not on vision but on design—to use the terms of his famous title, *Vision and Design. Then* we can see the beauty of African and Chinese art, having surrendered the misleading mimetic criteria so compelling to Hegel. Loosening the beauty-mimesis ligature made it possible for Fry to become a great formalist art critic, but because he continued to see the ligature between art and *beauty* as that of a necessary connection, so that of necessity art is always beautiful, it failed to occur to him, as a theorist, that whole artistic traditions have existed in which beauty was never the point at all. Beauty was not the rainbow that awaited us as the reward of sustained looking. It was never the case that the only proper way to address art was that of aesthetic contemplation at all. To put it another way, it never occurred to Fry, any more than it had occurred to Ruskin, that the beauty that was incontestably present in, for example, the great cathedrals, may have been a means rather than an end. The point was not to stand in front of the church and gape at the ornamentation, but to enter the church, the beauty being the bait, as it so often is in entering into sexual relationships.

Fry's one contemporary who appears to have understood this was Marcel Duchamp. In conversations that took place in 1967, Duchamp said: "Since Courbet, It's been believed that painting is addressed to the retina. That was everyone's error. The retinal shudder!" His argument is quite historical: "Before, painting had other functions, it could be philosophical, religious, moral. Our whole century is completely retinal, except for the Surrealists, who tried to go outside it somewhat." Duchamp, to whom I'll return, expressed this to Pierre Cabanne, but he had been almost unique in recognizing the deep conceptual disconnection between art and aesthetics in his readymades of 1913–1915 which, art-historically speaking, was just the right time for this to have reached consciousness as a philosophical possibility, when what we might call "The Age of Aesthetics" was drawing to a close, and our present age, which artistically owes so much to Duchamp, beginning, faintly, to dawn.

In 1905, ruminating on the somewhat farcical trial between Whistler and Ruskin that had entertained London audiences in 1879, Proust wrote that while Whistler had been right that there is a distinction between art and morality, on another plane Ruskin was right that all great art is morality." In 1903, as we saw, Moore seriously argued that the consciousness of beauty was among the supreme moral goods. We are safe, I think, in speaking of an atmosphere at the beginning of the twentieth century in which Rimbaud's image of abusing beauty could still have been seen as an abuse of morality. I can think of no more vivid a gesture of abusing beauty by abusing great art than Duchamp's 1919 work in which he drew a moustache on a postcard of Mona Lisa, and lettered a mild obscenity beneath that paradigm of art at its greatest. Like everything by Duchamp, this work is a field of fiercely competing interpretations, but I want to use it as an historical signpost of a deep change in attitude that calls for an historical explanation. I want to focus on an art-historical episode in the course of which, greatly to the benefit of the philosophical understanding of art, a logical space was definitively opened between art and beauty. It was a space that remained invisible to the members of Bloomsbury who, for all their modernist ideals, were essentially late Edwardians. It was invisible to them because they had the idea, expressed in Fry's dictum, that works of art, perceived as ugly, will ultimately be perceived as beautiful. In fairness, that was a dictum that continued to define what we might consider the a priori of artistic perception down to the threshold of our time. "All deeply original art," Clement Greenberg declared, "is initially perceived as ugly." "The highest responsibility of the artist is to hide beauty," John Cage said in his so-called Julliard Lecture in 1952, quoting W.H. Blythe's *Haiku*. It was a gap that remained invisible until the great conceptual efforts of the 1960s to define art. The opening of the gap is the contribution in my view of what I shall term the Intractable Avant-garde.

A Revolt Against Beauty

I want, in setting the scene for of my historical explanation, briefly to return to Moore's philosophy, and in particular to the connection between the two supreme goods he holds up for examination. Moore sees a clear connection between goodness and beauty. "It appears probable that the beautiful should be *defined* as that of which the admiring contemplation is good in itself" The two values, Moore claims, are so related to one another "that whatever is beautiful is also good." He goes further: "To say that a thing is beautiful is to say, not indeed that it is itself good, but that it is a necessary element in something which is: to prove that something is truly beautiful is to prove that a whole, to which it bears a particular relation as a part, is truly good." So Moore sees some near-entailments between art and beauty, and between beauty and goodness. "With regard to the question what *are* the mental qualities of which the cognition is essential to the value of human intercourse, it is plain that they include, in the first place, all those varieties of aesthetic appreciation which formed our first class of goods." With this, I think, Moore is seeking a connection between the cognition of beauty and the kind of human intercourse in which those for whom beauty is a value endeavor to participate. They will seek human intercourse with those who are exactly like them in highly prizing aesthetic experience. They will seek to form relations with those as much like themselves as possible—those whose "mental states," to use Moore's expression, are themselves good. And this indeed was the principle on which Bloomsbury friendship was based: It consisted almost entirely of those who assigned to beauty the highest moral priority. The Bloomsburys saw themselves as the true vessels of civilization.

And they perhaps supposed it the mark of a civilization that it create individuals of the sort they exemplified. In this, I think, they were not so far from Kant, in the light of his concluding proposition that beauty is the symbol of morality, even if connected, in his view, by way of a kind of analogy. Beauty, Kant writes, introducing an unlovely term from rhetoric, is an *hypotyposis* of morality, presenting moral concepts with a certain vividness and poetry. Kant observes that, "we often describe beautiful objects of nature or art by names that seem to put a moral appreciation at their basis. We call buildings or trees majestic and magnificent, landscapes laughing and gay, even colors are called innocent, modest, tender, because they excite sensations which have something analogous to the consciousness of the state of mind brought about by moral judgments." There is in aesthetic judgment, moreover, an entailed disinterestedness as well as a universality, which in Kant's philosophy was *sine qua non* for moral conduct. The person who values aesthetic experience has a moral fineness in that she or he is *enobled* through the disinterestedness. Remember, further, that Kant defined Enlightenment as mankind's coming of age—a cultural stage he would have believed the South Sea Islanders have not and perhaps for a long time will not have attained. And now the question was: how is it that just those nations defined by civilized high-mindedness should have made the most savage and protracted war that history up to that point had known?

It was with this question that the concept of beauty became abruptly politicized by avant-garde artists around 1915, which falls midway in the period of the readymades in Duchamp's career. It became that in part as an attack on the position, under which art and beauty were internally linked, as were beauty and goodness. And the "abuse of beauty" became a device for dissociating the artists from the society they held in contempt. Rimbaud became an artistic and moral hero—the poet everyone wanted to be. "I believe in the genius of Rimbaud," the young André Breton wrote Tristan Tzara, the author of the Dada Manifesto of 1918. It is Dada to which I primarily refer in the project of disconnecting beauty from art as an expression of moral revulsion against a society for whom beauty was a cherished value, and which cherished art itself because of beauty. Here is a recollective account by Max Ernst:

> To us, Dada was above all a moral reaction. Our rage aimed at total subversion. A horrible futile war had robbed us of five years of our existence. We had experienced the collapse into ridicule and shame of everything represented to us as just, true, and beautiful. My works of that period were not meant to attract, but to make people scream.

Ernst knew the war—he had been an artilleryman—and his art was aggressive, as his perception of the war-makers as hateful required it to be. In some measure this was true of German Dada in general. The First International Dada exhibition in Berlin had signs declaring that art was dead—"*Die Kunst ist Tot*"—adding "Long life to the *maschinen Kunst Tatlins*". Its members were not out to vilify German values—they were bent on destroying them by forcing upon German consciousness an art it could not swallow. Its means were a kind of aggressive foolishness. The original spirit of Dada was a kind of exaggerated play in the shadow of the war, a way of demonstrating by infantile actions its contempt for the clashing patriotisms: the term itself was baby-talk for "rocking horse," and the Zurich Dadaists registered their protests though buffoonery against what Hans Arp called "the puerile mania for authoritarianism which could use art itself for the stultification of mankind:"

While the thunder of guns sounded in the distance, we pasted, we recited, we versified, we sang with all our soul. We searched for an elementary art that would, we thought, save mankind from the furious folly of these times. We aspired to a new order.

And here is Tristan Tzara in the Dadaist Manifesto of July, 1918:

There is a great negative work of destruction to be accomplished. We must sweep and clean. Affirm the cleanliness of the individual after the state of madness, aggressive complete madness of a world abandoned to the hands of bandits, who rend one another and destroy the centuries.

Hence Tzara's dream to assassinate beauty.

Dada art was vehemently ephemeral—posters, book jackets, calligrams, pamphlets, recitations, as we would expect from a movement made of poets as well as artists. These ephemera, in their very ephemerality, were what Tzara celebrated as "means of combat." An exhibition of Dada art would consist of scraps of paper, yellowing snapshots, and a few sketches from the Café Voltaire in Zurich, where it all took place. Dada refuses to be found beautiful—and that is its great philosophical significance when we consider the consoling narrative that with the passage of time, what was rejected as art because not beautiful becomes enfranchised as beautiful and vindicated as art. This perhaps did happen with the avant-garde art of the nineteenth and early twentieth centuries. Matisse, for example, became for many a paradigm of beauty, as did the Impressionists so reviled in their time. I see Dada by contrast as the paradigm of what I am terming The Intractable Avant-Garde, the products of which are misperceived if perceived as beautiful. That is not its point or ambition.

From Taste to Disgust

The narrative of aesthetic redemption assures us that sooner or later we will see all art as beautiful, however ugly it appeared at first. *Try to see this as beautiful!* becomes a sort of imperative for those who look at art that does not initially appear beautiful at all. Someone told me that she found beauty in the maggots infesting the severed and seemingly putrescent head of a cow, set in a glass

FIGURE 7   Damien Hirst, *A Thousand Years*, 1990
    Try to see this as beautiful?

display case by the young British artist Damien Hirst. It gives
me a certain wicked pleasure to imagine Hirst's frustration if
hers were the received view. He intended that it be found disgusting, which was the one aesthetically unredeemable quality
acknowledged by Kant in the *Critique of Aesthetic Judgment*.
Disgust was noticed by him as a mode of ugliness resistant to the
kind of pleasure which even the most displeasing things—"the
Furies, diseases, the devastations of war"—are capable of caus-
ing when represented as beautiful by works of art. "That which
excites *disgust* [*Ekel*]," Kant writes, "cannot be represented in
accordance with nature without destroying all aesthetic satisfaction." The representation of a disgusting thing or substance has
on us the same effect that the presentation of a disgusting thing
or substance would itself have. Since the purpose of art is taken
to be the production of pleasure, only the most perverse of
artists would undertake to represent the disgusting, which cannot "in accordance with nature," produce pleasure in normal
viewers.

I don't know what works of art, if any, Kant could have had in
mind as disgusting, and he may have counted the very idea of disgusting art as incoherent: if a piece of mimesis was of something
disgusting, it would itself be disgusting, contravening its status as
art, which in its nature is meant to please. I have seen a sculpture

FIGURE 8 *The Prince of the World*, St. Sebald, Nürnberg, 1310
A high moral purpose, in poor taste

from Nuremberg from the late Gothic era, where a figure, known as "The Prince of the World," which looks comely and strong from the front, is displayed in a state of wormy decay when seen from behind: the body is shown the way it would look decomposing in the grave. Such sights explain why we actually bury the dead. It is intended thus to be seen as revolting by normal viewers, and there can be no question of what is the intended function of showing bodily decay with the skill of a Nuremberg stone carver. It is not to give the viewer pleasure. It is, rather, to disgust the viewer, and in so doing, to act as a *vanitas,* reminding us through presentation that the flesh is corrupt, and its pleasures a distraction from our higher aspirations, namely to achieve everlasting blessedness and avoid eternal punishment. To show the human body as disgusting is certainly to violate good taste, but Christian artists were prepared to pay this price for what Christianity regards as our highest moral purpose. One has, I suppose, a choice between denying that it is art since it contravenes taste, as I surmise that Kant would have done; or to dismiss taste as he and his contemporaries understood it as too narrow a criterion for defining art.

That we have no difficulty in acknowledging as art *The Prince of the World*—or even Damien Hirst's maggoty *tête de vache*—shows how far we now are from eighteenth-century aesthetics, and how complete a victory the Intractable Avant-Garde has achieved. Indeed, it has recently been argued by Jean Clair, a conservative French critic, that what Kant notices as a marginal case has become in contemporary art a "new aesthetic category" made up of "repulsion, abjection, horror, and disgust." Disgust, Jean Clair explains, is a "common trait, a family resemblance" of the art produced today "not only in America and Europe, but even in the countries of central Europe thrown open to western modernity." The French language permits a play on words between *goût* (taste) and *dégoût* (disgust) unavailable in English, which finds no such clear morphemic nexus between *taste* and *disgust.* It allows us to paraphrase Jean Clair's view of *la fin de l'art* as *the end of taste*—a state of affairs in which disgust now occupies the position antecedently occupied by taste. And this indeed, as Jean Clair sees it, expresses the sad decline of art over the past few centuries: "From taste . . . we have passed on to disgust."

My sense is that Jean Clair grossly overstates the case. There are, to be sure, those who derive a perverted pleasure in experiencing what the normal viewer finds disgusting: who have, one might say, "special tastes." James Joyce's hero, Leopold Bloom, who relished the faint taste of urine in his breakfast kidney, furnishes a mild example of what I have in mind. Andres Serrano, whose photograph, *Piss Christ,* became a talisman in the culture wars of the 1990s, made a less notorious photograph in a series he called *The History of Sexuality.* It shows a man lying down, his mouth opened to receive a stream of urine from a pretty woman standing over him. The act is associated with degradation, as indeed the use of urine is in *Piss Christ.* It belongs to the story of Christ's suffering—his passion—that he was subjected to the indignities Serrano's subject willingly pursues. But the affect of urine must remain associated with disgust or the pursuit of it loses any point. Artists interested in representing the disgusting would not have this special audience in view. Their aim is precisely to cause through their art sensations that, in Kant's phrase, "we strive against with all our might." Kant would have had no recourse but to regard this as the perversion of art. It would be of no value to such artists if a taste for the disgusting were to be normalized. It is essential to their aims that the disgusting remain disgusting, not that audiences learn to take pleasure in it, or find it somehow beautiful, which sounds like what Jean Clair claims has happened. Critics may applaud the use of disgust in contemporary art, not because they have a new aesthetic but because they applaud the use of it the artists make. But in view of the vehemence of Jean Clair's polemic, it is worth dwelling for a moment on the phenomenon of disgust in contemporary art.

"Disgusting" has a fairly broad use as an all-round pejorative, but it also and I think primarily, refers to a specific feeling, noticed by Darwin in his masterpiece, *The Expression of the Emotions in Man and Animals,* as "excited by anything unusual in the appearance, odor, or nature of our food." Evidence for the centrality of food "includes the facial expression, which focuses on oral expulsion and closing of the nares, and the physiological concomitants of nausea and gagging." It has little to do with literal taste. Most of us find the idea of eating cockroaches disgusting, but for just that reason few of us really knows how cockroaches taste. "A smear of soup in a man's beard looks disgusting, though there is of course nothing disgusting in the soup itself" is one of Darwin's examples. There is nothing disgusting in the sight of a baby with food all over its face, though, depending on circumstances, we may find it disgusting that a grown man's face should be smeared with *marinara* sauce. Like beautification, which I shall discuss later, disgust is one of the mechanisms of acculturation, and there is remarkably little variation in our schedules of what disgusts. So disgust is an objective component in the forms of life people actually live. The baby is very quickly taught to wipe its face lest others find it disgusting, and we hardly can forebear reaching across the table to remove a spot of chocolate from someone's face—not for their sake but for ours. What he speaks of as "core disgust" has become a field of investigation for Jonathan Haight, a psychologist at the University of Virginia. He and his associates set out to determine "the kinds or domains of experience in which Americans experience disgust." Foods, body products, and sex, not unexpectedly, got high scores when people were queried on their most disgusting experiences. Subjects also registered disgust in situations in which "the normal exterior envelope of the body is breached or altered." I was philosophically illuminated to learn that of the seventeen or so authenticated feral children, *none* evinced disgust at all. But I am also instructed by the fact that my cultural peers are disgusted by what disgusts me, more or less.

This overall consensus encourages me to speculate that most of us would unhesitatingly find disgusting the work of the widely admired artist, Paul McCarthy, which characteristically uses food in ways that would elicit disgust were we to see someone doing that in life, confirming Kant's observation. Consider what may be his masterpiece—the video of a performance titled *Bossy Burger,* which transpires in a hamburger stand, the interior of which is utterly nauseating, with dried splotches and piles of food pretty much everywhere. McCarthy, togged out in an initially immaculate chef's uniform and toque, wears the Alfred E. Newman mask that connotes imbecility, and his character grins his way through fifty-five minutes of clownishly inept food preparation. Thus he pours far more ketchup into a sort of tortilla than it can possibly hold, folds it over with the ketchup squishing out, and moves on to the next demonstrations. These involve milk and some pretty ripe turkey parts. The character is undaunted as his face, garments, and hands quickly get covered with what we know is ketchup but looks like blood, so he quickly takes on the look of a mad butcher. He piles the seat of a chair with food. He makes cheerful noises as he bumbles about the kitchen or moves to other parts of the set, singing, "I love my work, I love my work." I can hardly write about this piece without feeling queasy, and there can be little doubt that it is McCarthy's purpose to elicit disgust. He may, like the sculptor of *The Prince of the World*, have a larger purpose. He may, for example, intend to "debunk the false idealism [he] regards as rampant in Hollywood films, advertising, and folklore," as one commentator writes. His work may "relentlessly and rigorously probe the air-brushed innocence of family entertainment to reveal its seamy psychic underpinnings," to cite another critic. So it may, by virtue of what Kant calls hypotyposis in connection with beauty, show what really underlies it all, as the worm-riddled backside of *The Prince of the World* was intended to underscore our common mortality. But that does not erase the fact that maggots count as disgusting. So possibly McCarthy is a kind of moralist, and his works are really meant to awaken us to awful truths and their disgustingness is a means to edificatory ends. That leaves intact the revulsion their contemplation evokes. It does not erase the disgust.

A critic might, without redundancy, say that McCarthy's work is disgusting because it is disgusting. Its being disgusting, descriptively speaking, might give a reason, might even entail, that it is disgusting aesthetically, and as a matter of critical assessment. Once we open up the distinction between the use of the same term to appraise and to describe, McCarthy's enthusiasts would be entitled to say that it is beautiful because it is disgusting. The position of Dada, after all, could have been expressed as follows: It is disgusting because it is beautiful. That would be a way of saying that artists have no business making beautiful things for an immoral society! Max Ernst told Robert Motherwell that he and his fellow Dadaists once staged an exhibition of their art in a toilet.

It is a protraction of Bloombury imperatives, however, that moves McCarthy's commentators not so much to praise it for being disgusting, but to say instead that it must be descriptively beautiful after all. "I wanted to think about the question of beauty in your work," an interviewer murmured, "to move from the manifest to the latent." The *Times* speaks of the "unlikely beauty of the work," adding that it is "Not standard beauty, obviously, but a beauty of commitment and absorption." I have to believe that McCarthy's perceptions can be very little different from the rest of us. He has indeed almost perfect pitch for "disgust elicitors," and accordingly making the art he does must be something of an ordeal. That may have the moral beauty that undergoing ordeals possesses, especially when undertaken for the larger welfare. But if it is this sort of ordeal, it has by default to be disgusting, even if we find it "beautiful" that it is so. I find it inconceivable that he is aiming at beauty after all!

Abject Art

"Nothing is so much set against the beautiful as disgust," Kant wrote in his 1764 essay, *Observations on the Feeling of the Beautiful and the Sublime*. The sublime is too large a topic to address at this point in my inquiry, but it is worth noting that in that pre-critical text, Kant deliciously observes that the antonym of the sublime is the *silly*, which suggests that the effect of Dada was less the abuse of beauty than the rejection of the sublime. But just possibly the disgusting, as logically connected to beauty through opposition, can also have the connection with morality that beauty does. In the early 1990s, curators recognized a genre of contemporary art they designated "Abject Art," which may be what Jean Clair has primarily in mind. "The abject," writes the art historian Joseph Koerner, "is a novelty neither in the history of art nor in the attempts to write that history." Koerner cites, among other sources, a characteristically profound insight of Hegel: "The novelty of Christian and Romantic art consisted of taking the abject as its privileged object. Specifically, the tortured and crucified Christ, that ugliest of creatures in whom divine beauty became, through human evil, basest abjection." Rudolph Wittkower begins his great text on art and architecture in Italy after the Council of Trent by recording the decision of that council to display the wounds and agonies of the martyred, in order, through this display of affect, to elicit the sympathy of viewers and through that to strengthen threatened faith. "Even Christ must be shown 'afflicted, bleeding, spat upon, with his skin torn, wounded, deformed, pale and unsightly' if the subject calls for it." Hegel cites the art historian, Count von Rumohr on an earlier Byzantine tradition:

> Accustomed to the sight of gruesome physical punishments, [they] pictured the Saviour on the Cross hanging down with the whole weight of his body, the lower part swollen, knees slackened and bent to the left, the bowed head struggling with the agony of a gruesome death. Thus what they had in view as their subject was physical suffering as such. [By contrast] the Italians were accustomed to give a

comforting appearance to the face of the Saviour on the Cross, and so, as it seems, followed the idea of the victory of the spirit and not, as the Byzantines did, the succumbing of the body.

The tendency in the Renaissance to beautify the crucified Christ was in effect a move to classicize Christianity by returning the tortured body to a kind of athletic grace, denying the basic message of Christian teaching that salvation is attained through abject suffering. The aestheticism of the eighteenth century was a corollary of the rationalism of natural religion. It was Kant's stunning achievement to situate aesthetics in the critical architectonic as a form of judgment two small steps away from pure reason. Romanticism, as in the philosophy of Hegel, was a re-affirmation of the Baroque values of the Counter-Reformation. The problem with art, as Hegel saw it, lay in its ineradicable dependence upon sensuous presentation. As with the blood, the torn flesh, the shattered bones, the flayed skin, the broken bodies, the reduction of consciousness to pain and agony in Baroque representation. What Abject art has done is to seize upon the emblems of degradation as a way of crying out in the name of humanity. "For many in contemporary culture," the critic Hal Foster writes, "truth resides in the traumatic or abject subject, in the diseased or damaged body. Thus body is the evidentiary basis of important witnessings to truth, of necessary witnessings against power."

Down with the Alps!

In view of the history of human suffering which beyond question was the chief cultural product of the twentieth century, it is astonishing how dispassionate, how rational, how distancing, how abstract so much of twentieth-century art really was. How innocent Dada itself was, in its artistic refusal to gratify the aesthetic sensibilities of those responsible for the First World War—to give them babbling in place of beauty, silliness instead of sublimity, injuring beauty through a kind of punitive clownishness. The Intractable Avant-Garde's spirit of play—or even, if one wants to be censorious, of silliness—remains alive in art today.

Consider, for illustrative purposes, a marvelous exhibition that was installed in 1998 at the Kunsthaus in Zurich—a stone's throw from the old Café Voltaire where Dada originated—named after one of the whimsical "non-negotiable demands" of a student uprising there in the early 1980s: "Down with the Alps! *Ein frei Sicht zum Mittelmeer*—An uninterrupted View of the Mediterranean!" Initially a protest against rebuilding the municipal opera house, the riots escalated into an action militant enough to call for plastic bullets and tear gas, but imaginative enough to produce some crazy ideas, like demolishing the Alps to open up a free view of the Mediterranean: Razing the Alps was a metaphor for changing national identity ("Switzerland must be reinvented!") The demand is also pure Dada, as so many of the works in the show were. The exhibition's political subtext was to demonstrate through its art that Switzerland belonged to the same artistic culture as, say, Germany or the United States. That means that official artistic culture today is Dada through and through— which means in turn that virtually everything on view belonged to the Intractable Avant-Garde.

Neo-Dada no longer has the hope that it will reform the modern nation by abusing beauty. But perhaps by weakening if not destroying the supposedly internal relationship between art and beauty, it has made it possible for art more directly to address the inhumanities that so revolted the generation of artists after World War I. And this may explain the emergence of Abject Art as well as the sort of aesthetic that Jean Clair finds so distressing. The Intractable Avant-Garde did not really address the human body as the site of suffering and the object of political outrage.

Beauty and Other Aesthetic Qualities

I regard the discovery that something can be good art without being beautiful as one of the great conceptual clarifications of twentieth-century philosophy of art, though it was made exclusively by artists—but it would have been seen as commonplace before the Enlightenment gave beauty the primacy it continued to enjoy until relatively recent times. That clarification managed to push reference to aesthetics out of any proposed definition of art, even if the new situation dawned very slowly even in artistic consciousness. When contemporary philosophers of art, beginning with Nelson Goodman, set aesthetics aside in order to talk about representation and meaning, this was not done with the expectation that we will return to aesthetics with an enhanced understanding. It was done, rather, with the awareness that beauty belongs neither to the essence nor the definition of art.

But that does not mean that *aesthetics* belongs neither to the essence nor the definition of art. What had happened was that aesthetics had become narrowly identified with beauty, so that in ridding art of beauty, the natural inference was that we are in position to segregate the philosophical analysis of art from any concern whatever with aesthetics, all the more so since aesthetics was as much taken up with natural as with artistic beauty. The more reason, then, to put aesthetics to one side and concentrate on the philosophical questions of art, which had such deep affinities with the kinds of issues that appealed to philosophers, in the analysis of language and of science.

What the disgusting and the abject—and for the matter the silly—help us understand is what a heavy shadow the concept of beauty cast over the philosophy of art. And because beauty became, in the eighteenth century especially, so bound up with the concept of taste, it obscured how wide and diverse the range of aesthetic qualities is. Disgust, for example, provokes the viewer to feel revolted by what the work of art that possesses it is about. It does so in just the same way that eroticism arouses the viewer to be sexually attracted to the subject of the work. These observations are slightly simple-minded, of course. It may take considerable interpretation to see what the fact that it is disgusting *means* in a work of art. The purposes of eroticism in a work of art may be to get the viewer to think about his or her inhibited personality or emotionally impoverished life.

Cuteness in a work of art, exactly as in life, is a way of getting us to feel warm and protective toward what is seen to possess it. Given these kinds of examples, aesthetics may itself explain why we have art in the first place. We have it in order that our feelings be enlisted toward what the art is about.

What the Intractable Avant-Garde achieved, it seems to me, in addition to removing beauty from the definition of art by proving that something can be art without having beauty, was that art has had far too many aesthetic possibilities that it was distorting to think of it as though it had only one. I do not believe, with Jean Clair, that we have, with disgust, a new aesthetic, in which distaste replaces taste. We have, rather, a new appreciation of aesthetic possibilities, including a fresh way of thinking about beauty itself. Or at least of beauty as an aesthetic quality of art when it is beautiful. The difference between beauty and the countless other aesthetic qualities is that beauty is the only one that has a claim to be a value, like truth and goodness. The annihilation of beauty would leave us with an unbearable world, as the annihilation of good would leave us with a world in which a fully human life would be unlivable. But we may not lose a lot if artistic beauty were annihilated, whatever that means, because art has a number of other compensatory values, and artistic beauty is an incidental attribute in most of the world's artistic cultures. The pressing philosophical question then is what is the appropriate connection between art and beauty. And we might find some guidance in the rather clearer case of disgust. Disgust is clearer because what we are disgusted with in art is pretty much what we are disgusted with in reality. This is, if I may be excused, what is so beautiful in Kant's discovery that disgust cannot be disguised, so that when the disgusting is represented, its representation is as disgusting as what is represented. There is no temptation, then, to distinguish between the naturally and the artistically disgusting, as there is between natural and artistic beauty. To be sure, we may be disgusted with art because it happens to show disgusting things. The Flemish artist, Wim Deloye, made some bathroom tiles in which he pictured some very realistic turds. If we are disgusted with the art, it will be because we are disgusted by what the art is of. The photographer Ariane Lopez-Cuici made some photographs of what is medically designated a morbidly obese woman. People were not only disgusted with the photographs because they have been taught to be disgusted with fat, they were disgusted with Lopez-Cuici because she chose such models when there is no end of "beautiful," that's to say slender, models to chose from. But what is the relationship between natural and artistic beauty? I want to examine and even widen this question before addressing the place of beauty in the beautiful work of art.

1

3

Beauty and Beautification

The history of aesthetic reflection since the eighteenth century moves from a discourse in which it is not especially perceived as relevant to distinguish natural from artistic beauty, through the recognition that there is some kind of a boundary between them, to the perception that they are separated by a more or less vast and largely unmapped territory, sharing boundaries with natural beauty on the one side and artistic beauty on the other. Beauty of what we may speak of as the Third Realm plays a far greater role in human conduct and attitude than either of the (philosophically) more familiar kinds, since most persons have little occasion to think about the fine arts, or to gaze upon natural wonders, though what Kant speaks of as the starry heavens above may occasion awe and a sense of vastness in even the simplest of persons. By natural beauty it is perhaps best to think of beauty the existence of which is independent of human will, like the night sky or the sunset, mighty seas or majestic peaks. So the beauty of a garden would not be natural beauty, leaving it a question of whether it belongs to art or to the Third Realm. No one can be unaware of Third Realm Beauty in daily life, but the history of aesthetics, which has drawn examples from it, has often, perhaps typically, failed to note how different these are from either natural or artistic beauty.

Kant exemplifies the first moment of this history, as his choice of examples implies: he discusses green meadows just after discussing fine palaces, dissociating aesthetic judgment from whatever interest one may have in either. "A coat, a house, or a flower is beautiful," presumably in the same way; and Kant seems anxious that from the perspective of aesthetic analysis, no distinction is to

be drawn between flowers and floral decorations—"free delineations, outlines intertwined with one another." So "Nature is
beautiful because it looks like art," while "beautiful art must look
like nature," hence, from the perspective of beauty, in his scheme
at least, the distinction between art and nature does not greatly
signify. In this Kant was very much a man of the Enlightenment, a
period of cultivated taste, in which even the moderately affluent
were liberated from the urgencies of immediate interest to the possibility of a disinterested contemplation of natural beauties and
beautiful products of artistic genius. And the world was beginning
to feel safe enough for people to travel about, to see the Alps or
the artistic wonders of Italy.

Hegel defines the history's second moment, in that from the
outset he finds it crucial to distinguish sharply between artistic
beauty, on the one side, and "a beautiful color, a beautiful sky, a
beautiful river; likewise beautiful flowers, beautiful animals, and
even more of beautiful people." Artistic beauty is "higher" than
natural beauty, and "born of the spirit." Like natural beauty, artistic beauty "presents itself to *sense*, feeling, intuition, imagination."
But it does more than gratify the senses: when "fine art is truly art"
it "place[s] itself in the same sphere as religion and philosophy,"
bringing to our awareness "the deepest interests of mankind, and
the most comprehensive truths of the spirit . . . displaying even the
highest [reality] sensuously." At a minimum, art has a content that
must be grasped; it is, by contrast with skies and flowers, about
something. Of course, the distinction would be obliterated if one
thought of Nature as a Divine Visual Language, following Bishop
Berkeley or the painters of the Hudson River School, who saw
God addressing us through the medium of waterfalls or Catskill
cliffs. Moreover, the idea of content arises late in our understanding of art, at that point—which Hegel identifies as the end of art—
where art becomes a topic for intellectual judgment, rather than a
sensuous presentation of what is taken to be a reality. Art becomes
a topic for intellectual judgment when it enters the museum. In
the years in which Hegel was lecturing on aesthetics in Berlin,
Schinkel's *Altes Museum* (as it came to be called) was undergoing
construction nearby. Hegel was excited by the prospect of visiting
the collections, and seeing the development of the various schools
of painting historically. But he had a vivid sense of the difference
between a set of statues placed in a museum, and hence segregated

from life and treated as an object of study; and that same set of statues as part of a form of life in which they represent a pantheon of gods. In the latter role, they embody, for those who believe in them, the spirit of the gods themselves. They are the gods, so to speak, in the midst of those who worship them. When transferred to the museum, by contrast, they become objects of scholarly attention or connoisseurship, and their content a matter for art historical investigation.

There is in Hegel a kind of art which he mentions mainly to dismiss, as it does not qualify as a subject for "Science"—a term which in his usage has little to do with natural science, which is negligibly treated in his system. It designates, rather, "The Science of the *true* in its *true shape*," which is, after all, the way Hegel thinks of the processes through which Spirit arrives at an essential knowledge of its own nature. "Art can be used in fleeting play," he writes, "affording recreation and entertainment, decorating our surroundings, giving pleasantness to the externals of our life, and making other objects stand out by artistic adornment." Art so considered is not free but "ancillary"—it is *applied* to ends external to itself, whereas art *as* art is "free alike in its end and its means." It is only as such that it pertains, as with philosophy, to what he terms Absolute Spirit. Hegel is concerned to characterize art, which relies upon sensuous presentation, from thought. But there is a distinction to be made in regard to thought itself, which parallels entirely the distinction between fine and applied art: "Science may indeed be used as an intellectual servant for finite ends and accidental means" he concedes, and not for the high purposes of Science (with a capital S). This would have been expected from the consideration that art and thought are one, with the difference that art uses sensuous vehicles for conveying its content. In any case, Hegel has identified what I have pre-emptively designated as a third aesthetic realm, one greatly connected with human life and happiness. It is, in fact, coextensive with most forms of human life:

> Beauty and art does indeed pervade all the business of life like a friendly genius and brightly adorns all our surroundings whether inner or outer, mitigating the seriousness of our circumstances and the complexities of the actual world, extinguishing idleness in an entertaining way. . . . Art belongs rather to the indulgence and relaxation of the spirit, whereas substantial interests require its exertion.

> . . . Yet even though art intersperses with its pleasing forms everything from the war paint of the savages to the splendor of temples with all the richness of adornment, these forms themselves nevertheless seem to fall outside the true ends and aims of life.

Someone who thinks of art in these terms might consider it "inappropriate and pedantic to propose to treat with scientific seriousness what is not itself of a serious nature," as Hegel has set out to do in his *Lectures on Aesthetics*. I am not certain Hegel disagrees with this, despite his remarkably cosmopolitan personality. For it will not be as applied that he is to discuss art in the great work he has devoted to the subject. Like philosophical thought, art is a modality of free spirit. So there can be no question of "the *worthiness* of art" to be treated as philosophically as philosophy itself. Art is *worthy* of philosophical address only under the perspective of its highest vocation, which it shares with philosophy. So Hegel spends little time in exploring the territory he has uncovered, in which art is applied to the enhancement of life, even if it may, in certain periods, like the Renaissance, have been difficult to distinguish it from Art-capital-A. When Alberti was commissioned to give a new facade to Santa Maria Novella in Florence, was this upscale decoration or was it high art? We have such a problem today with the distinction between craft and art proper.

But the other border of the Third Realm is equally non-exclusionary, especially when we consider what Hegel singles out, under the head of beautiful people, the kind of beauty possessed by Helen of Troy, say, which we must suppose a wonder of nature. But Helen's choice of hairstyles, make up, or garment, would have belonged to the Third Realm, since it would have been chosen for enhancement, like the setting of a jewel. A great many of Kant's examples fall in this Third Realm—such as coats and gardens. These could not have been examples of free art in Hegel's thought, and this somewhat helps distinguish our own situation from that of our great predecessors.

In my own work, for example, I was from the first anxious to find a way of distinguishing real things from art works when there was no obvious way of doing so by examination, as in the case (my favorite!) of Brillo boxes and Andy Warhol's *Brillo Box*—a problem that did not and perhaps could not have arisen in Hegel's time. There was no way for a coat, for example, to be a work of art in

FIGURE 9
Marie-Ange
Guilleminot, *Le
Mariage de Saint-Maur
à Saint-Gall*, 1994
Meaning embodied

1828, as there is today, and subject to misuse if in fact used for the purposes of coats. In seeking to distinguish art works from what I termed "mere real things," I used *aboutness* as a principle of differentiation. It is a necessary condition for something to be an artwork that it be about something. Since something can possess aboutness without being art, more than content is accordingly needed to distinguish the artworks from mere real things. Aboutness, on the other hand, will not especially serve to distinguish art from applied art. Consider a wedding dress that was shown in the exhibition, discussed in Chapter 2, at the *Kunsthaus* in Zurich. It was by the French artist, Marie-Ange Guilleminot. It was not a work of art in the sense in which we praise wedding dresses generally as works of art—as marvelously designed, skillfully sewn and fitted, with appropriate rich fabrics and tasteful decorations. It was white, but rather plain and severe, and somewhat shroud-like. It could have been worn as a wedding dress, and was indeed so worn by the artist herself in a somewhat disturbatory performance work. We have reached a point in the history of art where there is no reason why a wedding dress—or a house dress, for that matter—cannot be a work of art, even if not a "work of art" in the commendatory vernacular sense in which we speak of the adorned bride herself as "looking like a work of art." What we are required to see is that Guilleminot's dress demands an interpretation, an ascription of meaning which explains its manifest properties. (It helps to know that she had sewn several kilos of lead under the skirt, perhaps to remind us of the weight, or burden, of marriage.) The dress was, and this idea is hardly un-Hegelian, what I have termed an *embodied meaning*. As a garment, the meaning of a wedding dress is its use: it is worn to be married in, and proclaims the purity of the wearer as well as the wealth of the bride's parents. That complex of symbolic uses is part of the meaning of the wedding dress as work of art, which is not itself intended to be used for anything but art. If someone actually wore Guillminot's dress *to be married in,* this would be close to what Duchamp termed a "reverse readymade," a little closer in this case to the art work reversed than his own example of using a Rembrandt for the purpose of an ironing board.

Part of what makes Kant's aesthetics so inadequate to the art of our time is that a work like this falls under neither of the kinds of beauty he distinguishes. It is neither free nor dependent. A (real) wedding dress has dependent beauty, in virtue of its connection with ritual and use. But as art it falls outside the domain of application entirely. Beauty is "free," according to Kant, when it "presupposes no concept of what the object ought to be." Kant uses as examples of free beauty that of flowers, birds, sea shells, but also of "delineations *à la grecque*, foliage for borders or wall papers." Interestingly, Kant classes "all music without words" as exemplifying free beauty. The beauty of a wedding dress, on the other hand, is quite clearly connected with a concept. The concept governs who wears it when and for how long a time and what it means that it be white and its wearer veiled. But a wedding dress as art is not covered by that same concept. Rather, *it* covers the concept, in that it absorbs it as part of its meaning. It is plain from this that Kant has no independent concept of beautiful art, since art possesses neither kind of beauty. What Kant lacks is the concept of meaning. Hegel requires art to have content if the parallels between it and philosophical thought hold, but his emphasis upon adornment, ornamentation, the refreshment of the spirit through objects of applied art overlooks the role that meanings play in the Third Realm: think, once more, of *Brillo Box* and the Brillo boxes. They have entirely different kinds of meaning, as I have demonstrated elsewhere. The concept of art is part of the meaning of the former, but it is not part of the meaning of the Brillo carton as applied, or as commercial art. It is somewhat interesting to observe that Hegel thinks aesthetically of the objects of the Third Realm from Kant's perspective of free beauty. They *please*, like sea shells and wallpaper borders, free from any concept and in themselves.

Nothing more sharply distinguishes the philosophy of art in Kant and in Hegel than the fact that *taste* is a central concept for Kant whereas it is discussed only to be dismissed by Hegel: "Taste is directed only to the external surface on which feelings play," he wrote. "So-called 'good taste' takes fright at all the deeper effects of art and is silent when externalities and incidentals vanish." As I have suggested, taste was, as much as reason, the defining attribute of the Enlightenment. In the *Analysis of Beauty*, Hogarth draws attention to the serpentine line, whether it characterizes a dancing master's leg or the leg of a chair, a woman's figure or the shape of a tea pot. Hogarth argues that anybody, and not just "painters and connoisseurs," know what good taste is—much as his contemporary, Bishop Berkeley, argued that "The illiterate bulk of mankind complain not of any want of evidence in their senses, and are out of all danger of becoming skeptics." Hogarth could argue this because English life embodied styles of dress, of decoration, and of craft to such a degree that an appropriately placed Englishman or Englishwoman would acquire taste as naturally as they would acquire their language. Or they could if they were situated in a fortunate social class, like their counterparts in Heian Japan, also a period of all but impeccable taste. All of this is absent from Hegel's analysis, and I consider this to be progress toward taking art seriously. The shift takes us from the sphere of the refinement of the senses to the sphere of meaning. The problem with Hegel's introduction of the Third Realm is that he tends to treat it from the eighteenth-century perspective rather than from that of the nineteenth century, where art is taken so seriously as to be coupled in solemnity with philosophy.

The Third Realm of Beauty

It is now time to address the Third Realm of beauty, which, though it embraces the domains of *Vanity Fair* and *Human, All Too Human*, has been the deer park of moralists and satirists down the ages, and only been taken *au serieux* by what in the past decade or so is labeled Cultural Studies. It has certainly received relatively little in terms of direct philosophical attention. *Relatively* little, since pride (in Aristotle, Hume, and Davidson) and shame (in Sartre and perhaps Kierkegaard) have generated a logical as well as a moralistic literature. It is as if philosophers, by shunning it, pay tacit homage to Hegel's thought that, since not entirely free, Third Realm beauty can have no claim to philosophical attention. It can certainly not be regarded as a displaced form of philosophy, as art in its "highest vocation" is claimed by Hegel to be. Third Realm beauty is the kind of beauty something possesses only because it was *caused* to possess it through actions whose purpose it is to *beautify*. It is the domain, in brief, of *beautification*. In this realm, things are beautiful only because they were beautified—and beautification has perhaps seemed, to a puritanical philosophical consciousness, to be—the term is Hegel's—*unworthy* of philosophical attention. Morality has always been of central philosophical concern, but discussions of manners, which Hobbes sneers at as "small morals," has barely been noticed. And this somewhat parallels the distinction between considerations of beauty as against beautification. The explanation of this perhaps goes back to the most ancient of philosophical distinctions—that between reality and appearances—in that almost invariably Third Realm practitioners are bent on changing the appearances of things in order to beautify or prettify them, without these changes penetrating what it really is: "Beauty is only skin-deep." Skills at inducing such changes are learned and applied by what in many languages are called *aestheticians* (or in English *beauticians*), and perhaps because beautification seems an exercise of frivolity, touching nothing fundamental or essential in those who pursue it, it is not difficult for philosophers to assimilate philosophical aesthetics as such to the study of beautification—to *aesthetics* as the practice of (for example) cosmetology—and hence to write the discipline off as having at best a marginal relationship to the True and the Good.

This would be, however, a piece of moral taxonomy, inasmuch as it expresses an unconscious disapproval of activities held to be unworthy of human beings. One gets a whiff of the grounds of such disapproval from Kant's remark on the use of a golden frame, "to merely recommend the painting by its *charm*." It is, Kant pronounces, "then called *finery* and injures genuine beauty." We can see exactly what Kant means when we consider the way modern curators often hold picture frames in contempt, and order their removal from around the paintings in their care. It is as if, instead of putting paintings in gold frames, we were to sew lace flounces around their edges, which would be—appealing to Webster on finery—"dressy or showy," and hence an insult to the art. Finery is intended to produce a certain effect, hence it really is akin to rhetoric, the skills of which are bent on making the case look worse or better than it is. "Finery," "dressiness," "show"—these are expressions of moralistic disapproval, and in a way they imply an underlying imperative, that people should not appear other than the way God made them. Hence Kant's contempt for tattoo-covered bodies, when the body—after all the image of God—is already as beautiful as it can be. The imperative is expressed in sumptuary codes, the purpose of which is not merely to regulate conduct since all codes have that purpose, but to control any propensity to extravagance or luxury. And of course to mislead viewers, who believe one's presented beauty to be one's own rather than due to artifice.

Beautification as a modality of moral self-consciousness presupposes a fairly complex epistemology and a metaphysics of the self, which may be made explicit by referring to the role the mirror image plays in its transactions. We look into the mirror not merely to see how we look, but how we expect others to see us, and, unless amazingly self-confident, we attempt to modulate our appearances in order that others shall see us as we hope to be seen. Happiness and unhappiness in this world are indexed to our appearances—which is perhaps why we have a concept of Heaven as a world in which happiness is not so indexed, since God sees us as we are without reference to how we appear. Sees us "for ourselves alone and not [our] golden hair," as Yeats puts it in a wry poem.

If we assimilate our concept of art to the concept of beautification, then, Hegel writes, "it is not itself of a serious nature," though it can have serious consequences.

> On this view, art appears as a superfluity, even if the softening of the heart which preoccupation with beauty can produce does not altogether become deleterious as downright effeminacy. From this point of view, granted the fine arts are a luxury, it has frequently been necessary to defend them in their relationship to practical necessities in general and in particular to morality and piety, and since it is impossible to prove their harmlessness, at least to give grounds for believing this luxury of the spirit may afford a greater sum of advantages than disadvantages.

I expect that the decision to establish a National Endowment for the Arts might have been justified by appeal to such considerations—that even if taxpayers ought not be asked to support luxury, an argument is available according to which art conduces to a certain softening of the human material. The ground disappeared from under this justification when the Endowment supported art which seemed to have the opposite moral effect, and the question, "Why should we support art perceived as *harmful* to the fabric of political society?" could not be avoided.

What is evident through this entire discussion, then, is that the very existence of a third aesthetic realm is internally related to moral considerations in a way in which art in its "highest vocation" is not, nor nature in its aspect as beautiful. Both of these, of course, can entail imperatives, especially when it becomes evident that preservation is in order when beauty is threatened. We cannot take it for granted that the beauties of nature or of art will be joys forever. But beautificatory practices themselves intersect every step of the way with various particular moral imperatives, which specify what we might call the bounds of taste (whose realm this is), viz, that something is too plain, or too ornate, or whatever. These aesthetic complaints can be, and typically are, over-ridden by moral considerations. When Kant wrote disapprovingly of ornamenting a church, it was perhaps his view that ornament was inconsistent with the momentousness of something being the house of God— as if the architects were bent on flattery by adding carving, let alone images. Consistently, it would similarly be prohibited to wear fine clothes to religious service, as if the church were, like a ball, the scene of flirtations or seduction. (There is a passage in *The Pillow Book* of Lady Sei Shonogun where she complains that a Buddhist monk is too good looking for the exercise of piety, through his looks drawing her to the world from which his preaching is to liberate her. So beware handsome priests and beautiful nuns!)

God, it might be said, was not quite so austere in his tastes. There is a famous candelabrum in the Bible, one which a curiously finicky God orders Moses to construct. It is a very ornate candelabrum for what after all was a desert people, but it was to be placed in a sanctuary fit for God, and to represent an offering and a sacrifice on the part of the children of Israel "that I might dwell among them." The candelabrum was to be made of pure gold, and God specifies its structure in a brief sufficiently detailed that it might be in a contract with a goldsmith:

> Of beaten work shall the candlestick be made: his shaft and his branches, his bowls, his knops, his flowers, shall be of the same.
> And six branches shall come out of the sides of it: three branches of the candlestick out of the one side, and three branches of the candlestick out of the other side:
> Three bowls made like unto almonds, with a knop and a flower in one branch; and three bowls made like almonds in the other branch, with a knop and a flower: so in the six branches that come out of the candlestick.
> And in the candlestick shall be four bowls made like unto almonds, with their knops and flowers.
> And there shall be a knop under two branches of the same, and a knop under two branches of the same, according to the six branches that proceed out of the candlestick.
> Their knops and branches shall be of the same: all it shall be one beaten work of pure gold.
> And thou shalt make the seven lamps thereof: and they shall light the lamps thereof, that they may give light against it.

The specification goes on, and it is clear that God means for the sanctuary, in which the candelabrum is to be placed, to be a simulacrum of God's own dwelling.

By the testimony of *Exodus,* God was not an aesthetic minimalist. A candelabrum of the sort he demands placed a serious burden on his subjects, which meant that it was perceived as a sacrifice. And we see, in religious custom, practices entirely opposite to the puritanism of Prussia. It is not uncommon to create highly ornamental frames for certain holy pictures, not, as Kant says about golden frames, to recommend the painting, which needs no recommendation, but to pay homage, in the only way one knows how to, to the being of whom it is the picture—a *bambino sacro,* the merciful Madonna, or the *nothilfige* saints to whom thanks are due for benign interventions. Appreciation is expressed through sometimes massive ornamentation, well beyond the boundaries of good taste and across into the boundaries of what we might consider bad taste, like lace on the wedding dress when it crosses a border into *froufrou.* The ornamental frame of the Pentecostal church has no business being tasteful because it has no business being bounded by the limits of good taste. If it is not too much then it is too little. The decorative programs of Flamboyant Gothic are quite clearly at odds with the anti-decorative program of Modernism, as in the writing of Adolf Loos—and in the architectural practice of Ludwig Wittgenstein—both of whom would have endorsed Kant's association of austerity with piety. The philosophical point, however, is that the exercise of taste is associated with how people believe they ought to live. Taste is not the mere application of discernment and fine discrimination. It belongs to ritual. If one thinks about it, church architecture belongs to applied religion, and differs from it as applied art differs from art "in its highest vocation," or as (continuing to follow Hegel) to applied in contrast with pure thought. Each of the three moments of Absolute Spirit in fact has a practicum in the Third Realm where human life is actually lived. And every practice is connected with some vision of what a human life ought to be.

Let us consider from this perspective Kant's example of a figure "adorned" with spirals "as the New Zealanders do with their tattooing." Hegel mentions body painting, as we saw, but has, so far as I can tell, no special attitude toward it other than as a primitive form of beautification, a misguided form of gilding the lily. For

Kant, by contrast, the human form is like the form of a church. As the handiwork of God, it cannot be improved upon. It needs no finery, though his discussion of coats suggests that he was thinking of good tailoring and gold buttons. For both philosophers, anthropological knowledge exceeds anthropological understanding. Neither, for example, understands what it means painstakingly to cover the surface of the body with regular circular lines by tattooing—or to paint the body in ways Hegel must have seen in engravings of Africans or Native Americans. This cannot, I think, strictly be considered beautification. It cannot because the paint or pattern serve important functions of a symbolic or magical kind. They involve ordeals for the sake of the power they confer. They connect the person who bears them to the greater forces of the universe: to spirits and deities. Taste has no application, though obviously ornamentation can be overdone. A heavily ornamental *mazuzzah* can in principle confer no higher power than the plainest of *mazuzzahs*. If it did, then all *mazuzzahs* should possess it. So it has to be gratuitous, which is what moralism holds in regard to beautification generally. It is mere luxury, toward which we can, with Kant, be negative or with Hegel be indifferent, or with Philip Johnson (when he fitted a pediment to the AT&T Building) be positive. These are competing philosophies of taste which, in a cosmopolitan culture such as our own, exist side by side. Theories of taste, however, are not matters of taste: they bring with them entire philosophies of conduct and of life. The ornamentation of a Hindu statue or of a miraculous icon can be painful to a disapproving minimalist, just as the latter's austerity can be criticized as lack of gratitude for favors conferred. So the absence or presence of ornament always transcends questions of aesthetics alone. And this will be true of the enhancement of human beings, where the no-make-up look proclaims, or can proclaim, commitment to the view that 'tis a gift to be simple. Beautification may accordingly also carry symbolic weight, which can be perverted if something is used for looks alone. Were the long locks of the Chasidim to be accepted merely as coiffeur, as in "The Chasidic Look," they would for those who take them up as fashion not have any symbolic weight at all, and certainly would not express the commitment to an entire form of life which the Chasidim are presumed to have made. There would be a difference between circumcision "because it looks better" and circumcision as a condition for entering the covenant with God. Perhaps nothing cosmetic is without symbolic meaning.

In discussing human beauty, Kant does not suppose that there is a single model for it, since he has become aware of racial differences, and recognizes that the different races will have non-congruent conceptions of human beauty. For any given race, the idea of a beautiful person, physiognomically considered, is the product of a kind of unconscious averaging, a statistical composite of the productive imagination which specifies a norm which "is at the basis of the normal idea of the beauty of the [human figure.]" as Kant writes in Section 17 of his *Critique*. There are now computer programs which are capable of extracting the norm from as many images as one cares to scan into one's machine. The resultant morph is unlikely to match any individual we may encounter, and it is similarly unlikely that an individual human being will perfectly exemplify the prevailing idea of beauty. In fact, it has recently been demonstrated that a consolidated image of perhaps sixty people will be voted more attractive than the images of most of those who participated in the consolidation. But as a morph it will coincide with the idea of beauty at which everyone with a comparable degree of experience will have arrived. It is, within certain limits to be discussed shortly, universal, without corresponding to reality. To the degree that we appreciate symmetry and regularity as the co-ordinates of beauty, they really do define a norm which actual persons fall away from by various degrees, to the point where genuine ugliness attaches to asymmetry or irregularity. (One of the problems of living in a world where human beings are represented who are closely conforming to the norm, as in television, is that the rest of us feel inadequate or even villainous!) The limits on universality are set by the circumstance that the norm of beauty will vary from society to society, especially insofar as each society consists of members of a distinct racial type: "Thus," Kant writes, "necessarily under these empirical conditions a Negro must have a different normal idea of the beauty of the [human figure] from a white man, a Chinaman a different normal idea from a European, etc. . . . It is the image for the whole race."

There were probably very few "Chinamen" or "Negroes" in most European centers in Kant's time, but Koenigsberg, where he spent his entire life, was a Hanseatic port, and he had ample opportunity to practice comparative physiognomy. I would surmise that if the averaging crossed racial lines—if the morphing operation were extended to cover the Caucasian, the Negro, and the Oriental racial types—there would be a kind of hypermorph which members of various races might pick out as beautiful, invariantly as to questions of racial identity. This is an entirely empirical matter: recently some computer-enhanced images of racially undifferentiated female heads were deemed most beautiful by both Western and Japanese males. And by now, perhaps, through television and cinema, everyone has seen everything.

One supposes, if beautification is the aim, that everyone would want to approach the hypermorph in looks. Kant cites a work of Polycleitus, the *Doryphorus* or *Spear-carrier*, which came to be known as the *Canon*, inasmuch as it so perfectly embodied the correct proportions of the ideal male form as to serve as an atlas for sculptors. But normic beauty is curiously bland: an authority writes that "balance, rhythm and the minute perfection of bodily form . . . do not appeal to us as they did to the Greeks of the Fifth Century." Kant himself is anxious to press the point that we must "distinguish the *normal idea* of the beautiful from the *ideal*," which—uniquely in the case of human beings—lies in the expression of *moral* qualities. "This shows that a judgment in accordance with *such a standard can never be purely aesthetical and that a judgment in accordance with an ideal is not a mere judgment of taste*." So ideal beauty may involve a trade-off between normic beauty and the expression of what Kant enumerates as "goodness of heart, purity, strength, peace, etc.—visible as it were in bodily manifestations (as the effect of that which is internal)." Hegel characterizes Romantic Art as responsive to the demand for making inwardness visible, of showing what a person is so far as that person is coincident with his or her feelings. And that would explain why *The Spear-carrier* is bland: classical art, if Hegel is right, had no concept of inwardness. It explains as well why a contemporary artist, Orlan, who submits herself to plastic surgery in order to make herself conform to aesthetic prototypes, in fact looks, well, creepy. She shows no inwardness. And it explains why the life-likeness induced by mortuary intervention underscores the death of the body— even if the face is given a happy smile. It also explains, I think, why the case presented to Socrates by Adeimanthus in the *Republic* is less readily imagined than one might believe: a perfectly unjust man who appears to be perfectly just. We can, within limits, feign looks, but not consistently. The kind of person we are shows through the kind of person we appear to be, there is a limit to the possibilities of expressional cosmetics, of making ourselves look kind or thoughtful or sensitive. Someone may feel that the reason they are unloved is because they appear too fat, which may be true or false—true under the criterion of normic beauty, false under that of inner beauty, which may alert others to the fact that someone is cruel or vacuous, or their opposites. Kant is entirely right in his suggestion that inner beauty is not a matter of taste alone, as that is exhibited in adolescents, who fall in love with football heros and prom queens, or by tycoons who marry models, whom they display as trophies. Inwardness sets a limit to how far hair transplants, nose jobs, liposuction, breast implants and the like will carry one. But the literature of moralists and cynics, back to ancient times, is replete with applicable wisdom, whether or not it shows up in classical art.

There is a certain set of political considerations involved in beautification, which would not, I think, have shown up in this literature, inasmuch as they only began to enter consciousness in relatively recent times. They arise when members of a certain group begin to think that they have sought to conform to a norm of beauty which in fact was imposed upon them by a politically dominant class—by men in the case of women, or by whites in the case of blacks, or, a—somewhat weaker case—by Gentiles in the case of Jews. As a corollary of contemporary feminism, it occurred to women that they aspired to an ideal of beauty which had been imposed upon them by men; or to blacks that they aspired to conform to a standard of beauty which in fact belonged to whites. When the possibility of imposition became a matter of a raised consciousness, beautificatory practices changed abruptly. In the case of African-Americans, even as militant a figure as Malcolm X went through a period in which he underwent a hair-straightening procedure, at considerable cost in pain, but felt to be worth it if in the end he would be perceived as not possessing the tight curls identified with negritude. So he would consider himself in terms of hair non-Negro (soft curls would be consistent with that). Hair is a very charged bodily part in black culture, mainly because kinked hair is part of the Negro stereotype—or would turn up in the averaging which defines the norm for the race, on Kant's view. But with the recognition that they had been applying a norm to themselves that was not their own, kinked hair became something to be proud of (and a black born with straight hair might have recourse to negrification of this feature.) The Afro hairstyle became a weapon in the aesthetico-racial wars: it flaunted what under prevailing norms would have been held to be disfiguring, by others and by oneself, so long as one subscribed to the racial status quo. "Black is beautiful" is a political refusal not to be oppressed aesthetically. That is a return to Kant's distinctions; it entails accepting a norm of beauty specific to the race. Black culture radiated out from cosmetic changes: the choice of African names, the wearing of African costumes, changing ones religion from Christianity to Islam. The moral quandary of a black person who looks white is the perduring theme of Adrian Piper's art.

The case of feminism is different in certain ways, in that there was not a time in which women sought to define feminine beauty in terms of male beauty—though flattened breasts in the 1920s served to reduce to invisibility a traditionally feminine attribute. Women sought—and by the evidence of the literature they still seek—to define female beauty as men are perceived to define it, and hence become what men want them to be. Co-eval with the Afro was the ritual bra-burnings, in which a garment identified with femininity, and which served to construct a female figure along certain lines, was cast out and women's natural contours were flaunted. Breasts were allowed to swing freely, nipples to show through tee-shirts. And, collaterally with the emergence of a politicized black culture, a politicized female culture appeared through which women sought to live in conformity with their own sexual reality as they perceived it, in which beauty as previously specified was now perceived as a trap.

None of this will be unfamiliar to anyone who lived through the later decades of the twentieth century, nor is it unfamiliar in the forms it assumes today. It is certainly subject to satire and caricature, but there can be little doubt that the struggle over whose canon of beauty we are to apply to ourselves goes well beyond what Kant described as taste, and well beyond the expression of moral states he felt must be adjoined to it. In a way which I shall leave until a later occasion to examine, not allowing one's self-definition to be imposed from without is close enough to what Kant thought of as autonomy to suggest that there is a deep connection between the aesthetics of the Third Realm and the realm of ethics.

It is to reject a categorical imperative in regard to how we shall appear, and to endorse one restricted to who we are in terms of race and gender—and such other facticities as may in the course of time emerge politically. This has its dangers, and, especially in the case of women, it has some far from well understood limits. The differences between races, while accounted for through evolution, is not required for human evolution. It is a difference more connected with variation than with speciation. With sexual difference, on the other hand, there has thus far been a bimorphic basis for generation. And this shows up in the role of sexual attraction. The human male is so constituted that he must be aroused, or there will be no erection, hence no pregnancies, hence no survival of the species. Feminine beauty is thus connected with the power to arouse and excite—and reproduce—and the now legendary "male gaze" is an agency of evolution.

This, of course, can change if the replenishment of the species can be detached from the psycho-chemistry of arousal. Viagra still requires sexual stimulation, but almost certainly there will be erectile prosthetics which dispense with this atavism, allowing the erection to be a matter of will, thus reproducing what Saint Augustine proposes was the condition of Adam before the Fall, able to plant his seed without the storms of passion. No longer under the imperatives of attractiveness, the human female will be free to appear as she cares to, indifferent to what turns men on. It is far from plain, moreover, that post-Adamic methods of impregnation are written into the genome. With cloning and the like, we can imagine and perhaps even foresee a time when men are sexually required only for sexual pleasure—or might even be cloned out because of social disorders blamed on testosterone. We are entering a brave new world, and Third Realm aesthetics gets less and less frivolous every day.

The Paradigm of Beautification

Part of Dada's heritage has been a distrust of beauty, at least in art. If beauty was not actively hated, there was at least a corollary attitude: Better the art be disgusting than beautiful. The pursuit of beauty in terms of personal looks, by contrast, is the aim of a major industry. In an interview conducted shortly before her untimely death, the innovative sculptor Eva Hesse grew almost shrill in declaring her distaste for beauty—for "prettiness"—in art. But as

FIGURE 10 Eva Hesse, with her *Expanded Expansion*, 1969
Shunning beauty as distasteful

we know from her diaries, she was preoccupied with her own beauty as a woman. When Kant opposed beauty with disgust in his early text "Observations on the Feeling of the Beautiful and the Sublime," he was thinking that the last thing a woman—Kant inevitably shared his era's attitudes toward gender—who aspires to be thought beautiful would want is to be found disgusting. This may seem a long way from the philosophy of art, but the term "aesthetics" is used in many cultures for the kind of ministrations on offer in what in American English we call "beauty shops." A young instructor in a Canadian university once told me that whenever she sees a position in aesthetics advertised by a philosophy department, she cannot suppress the thought that they are looking for someone able to do nails. And the question is whether we are dealing with different concepts of beauty, as the idea of three realms implies, or if there is not a greater unity here than at first appears.

In eighteenth-century philosophy, all three realms were obviously enough connected, which is why Kant was able to treat the three domains as one. Since painting was understood as mimetic, beautiful paintings were understood as paintings of beautiful scenes and beautiful persons. Persons of taste were eager to be surrounded with beautiful objects as a matter of course, which meant that if they collected paintings, they would be beautiful paintings, which in consequence meant specifically paintings of beautiful things—of things that looked beautiful in the same sense of "looking beautiful" that we have been canvassing here. However marginal beautification has been in philosophical aesthetics, it was the central concept in Kant's philosophy, which saw no special reason to provide a different analysis for natural and artistic beauty. Third Realm aesthetics was aesthetics as such—but beautification was the paradigm. So the discussion of this chapter was less an interlude than a preparation for addressing the question of what importance beauty can have in art, after its abuse at the hands of the Intractable Avant-Garde. This will be the topic in the next chapter.

4

Internal and
External Beauty

On Renaissance principles, paintings were windows on the world, pure transparent openings through which one saw what one would have seen standing outside, looking at what the picture instead showed. So a picture drew its beauty from the world, ideally having none of its own to contribute to what one saw, as it were, through it. This of course overlooks the contribution of the frame, as shaping the way the world presents itself through pictures to the eye. The stereotypical painter crooks the index finger against the thumb, framing the world until it resolves itself into a picture—until it looks the way she wants her picture to look—like Lily Briscoe in *To the Lighthouse*, or, we imagine, any of the Bloomsbury painters—Roger Fry and Vanessa Bell among others—scouting the south of France for what the traditional art schools designated *motifs*. Kant was famously a stay-at-home, but he lived in an era of aesthetic tourism. The well-to-do went abroad to see the sights: the Alps, the Bay of Naples, as well, of course, as the Piazza San Marco, the Pantheon, the Leaning Tower, the Acropolis. A pictorial industry grew up to provide souvenirs—objective memories—of what one had seen. This I take to be the background of Kant's somewhat surprising remark, cited but not discussed above, at §45 of the *Critique of Judgment*: "Nature is beautiful because it looks like art," when one would have expected the opposite instead. Kant seems to be saying that the world is beautiful when it looks the way painters represent it, when one thought they represented it because it was beautiful in the first place, if we understood rightly the Renaissance idea that the beauty we see pictured on the canvas or the panel is, since the picture is a pure transparency with nothing of its own to contribute, the sum-total of the picture's beauty.

One encounters this concept of pictorial transparency in discussions of the aesthetics of photography today. Roger Scruton writes: "If one finds a photograph beautiful, it is because one finds something beautiful in the subject." It is difficult to see how this account will survive the admittedly overdetermined case of Robert Mapplethorpe's photographs. As we saw earlier, Mapplethorpe's photographs were artistically faulted, by his modernist contemporaries, through the fact that they were hopelessly beautiful, though in the view of the general public they were objectionable, or even disgusting, because of their explicit sexual content. In *Civilization and Its Discontents,* Freud wrote that beauty's "derivation from the realms of sexual sensation is all that seems certain; the love of beauty is a perfect example of a feeling with an inhibited aim." On the other hand, Freud continues, "the genitals themselves, the sight of which is always exciting, are hardly ever regarded as beautiful." If Freud is right, we only get beauty if we do not depict the site of sexual pleasure directly. Mapplethorpe can be seen as endeavoring to overcome this by beautifying the way genitals are shown, to achieve images that are beautiful and exciting at once: pornography and art in the same striking photographs. "There are two distinct roads in photography," according to an early writer, Charles Caffin: "The utilitarian and the aesthetic: the goal of one being a record of facts, and of the other an expression of beauty." Caffin thought that photography as a fine art (the title of his book) "will record facts but not as facts," and he doubtless had in mind the model of Pictorialism—taking pictures which looked as much as possible like tonalist paintings such as those of Inness and perhaps Whistler. Mapplethorpe's X Portfolio images are fusions of the pornographic picture and the kind of photographic elegance he found in Steichen and Photo Secessionist camera work, which he admired in the exhibition *The Painterly Photograph*, organized by his friend John McKendrie, at the Metropolitan Museum in 1973. Before that, he could not see how photography could be an art, perhaps thinking that photography was essentially documentary, to use Caffin's term. His new aim, as he put it, was to "play with the edge" between art and pornography. It takes a certain suspension of moralist attitude to see a Polaroid, which Mapplethorpe devoted to his own engorged penis, held erect like a blunt club by means of a leather loop around his testicles, in the same aesthetic terms as the Photo-Secessionist masterpieces in *The Painterly Photograph*, say Steichen's exquisite *Flatiron Building*. But that was the paradox of his achievement—to show what one can sometimes barely stand to look at in photographs so beautiful one can hardly takes one's eyes off them. He was as obsessed with beauty as he was with his special approach to sex, and his aim throughout was to fuse these disparate obsessions.

The age of photography was not to begin for half a century after Kant wrote his text on aesthetics. Its inventor, Fox Talbot, because of his acknowledged deficiencies as a draftsman, sought a way in which Nature would transcribe *itself*, without the mediation of an artist: the photographic camera was, in his words, "Nature's pencil." The camera was built on Renaissance principles, which is why, until the invention of digitalization, photographs performed forensic roles. The camera was like an eye-witness. So if one aimed at beautification, one was obliged to beautify the object of the photograph, and then record that, which Mapplethorpe did in part with lights and shadows. Thus the theory of pictorial transparency survives.

This cannot, however, have been the whole story, not even for Kant, who recognized that art was capable of representing as beautiful the most paradigmatically ugly things. So the picture must somehow contribute to its beauty, since such motifs have none. It is here that Kant makes his parenthetical observation on disgust, as the "one kind of ugliness which cannot be represented in accordance with nature without destroying all aesthetic satisfaction, and consequently *artificial beauty*." I emphasize "artificial beauty." It is what I have been calling "beautification"—aesthetic sophism, making the worse appear better, which involves cosmetics, fashion, interior decoration, and the like, where we are not dealing with natural but with enhanced beauty. In the eighteenth century, in France especially, a close parallel was drawn between painting pictures and painting faces, so that, in his portrait of *Madame Pompadour at Her Vanity*, which shows the great lady with her rouge-brush before a mirror, François Boucher is virtually saluting a fellow artist. With the made-up face, Kant's follow-up thought would be exact—"we are conscious of it as art while yet it looks like nature." It looks like nature in nature's most aesthetically striking instances. So it is a kind of visual falsification—a trap for the unwary.

FIGURE 11   François Boucher, *Madame Pompadour at Her Vanity*, 1758
Applying is lying.

The French term for "to make up" is "farder" or "to color"
which explains in part why there was a traditional mistrust of colors—why Descartes went so far as to say we really did not need our
eyes to know what the world was like, since the blind can feel the
outlines and know the shapes of things. Ruskin appears to have had
beautification—or artifice—in mind when, in support of the
British Pre-Raphaelites, he condemns pretty much the entire his-

tory of painting from the time of Raphael down. In the first of two letters to *The Times* in 1851, Ruskin wrote that his young protégés

> desire to represent, irrespective of any conventional rules of picture making; and they have chosen their unfortunate though not inaccurate name because all artists did this before Raphael's time, and after Raphael's time did *not* do this, but sought to paint fair pictures rather than represent stern facts, of which the consequence has been that from Raphael's time to this day historical art has been in acknowledged decadence.

It did not incidentally matter that the reality was only imagined—"made up" by the artist in the other sense of the expression—that it was "false" in the sense that it did not exist, so long as if it did exist, it was not falsified in the interests of beautification.

Inevitably, the camera served as model for Ruskin's disciples. With the American Pre-Raphaelites, committed to Ruskin's agenda of visual truth, the highest accolade a painting could be paid was that it looked as if it were done with a camera. My sense is that appeal to photography was the arbiter even with the British Pre-Raphaelites—that like their American counterparts, their paintings were to be praised as transparent, as if they had been done by a camera, in the spirit of documentation. They were not "fair" but truthful pictures.

Deliberately "aesthetic" photography entered the discourse with Pictorialism, where Stieglitz and his peers tried to make photographs look beautiful (and by Ruskin's criterion, false) by making them look like paintings. But painting itself had changed. It has become, so to say, *Post-Raphaelite*. It had abandoned transparency—it was something to see in its own right, rather than something to see through. It was not abstract—it had recognizable subjects. But it created an atmosphere for them by absorbing them, one might say, into the paint. A movement had begun which would culminate in Abstract Expressionism where it was possible for paint to be its own subject. When Mapplethorpe complained that photography was not an art, he was not using painting as his model, much as he admired the Pictorialists who did. His teachers at Pratt were inculcated with Abstract Expressionist ideas, but *his* idea of the model artist was Duchamp. Abstract Expressionism did not and would not have allowed him to "play with the edge." But this takes me ahead of my story.

., Modernist paintings that Roger Fry featured in his two
ıtions at the Grafton Gallery were done midway in the tra-
ory from Manet to, let us say, Jackson Pollock and Franz Kline.
ıransparency could hardly be attributed to them. If they were
beautiful, that could neither be attributed to the beauty of their
subjects—since there was no way of telling what the subjects really
looked like from the pictures—nor to beautification. We could take
Picasso's word that the woman depicted in *Ma Jolie* was indeed
jolie—but the painting itself showed no evidence that she was. So
if the works were beautiful, it would have to be in some way other
than through showing a beautiful subject, or by beautifying
through artistic intervention a subject that was less than beautiful.
Art criticism needed to find these new ways. Fry more or less
delayed the search by insisting that they were really beautiful, but
difficult. In this chapter my aim will be to show how to use the
concept of beauty with a clearer sense of art-critical responsibility
than has thus far been the case. And at the same time I shall blur
the boundaries between the three realms of beauty addressed in
Chapter 3.

Seeing Beauty that Isn't There

When Matisse exhibited his startling *Woman with Hat* to wide
derision in 1905, he was approached by a German artist who asked
what was the actual color of Madame Matisse's dress when she sat
for this portrait. Matisse impatiently replied "Obviously black."
What could he have meant by "obviously"? Perhaps only that
women in Madame Matisse's class wore black as a matter of course.
That would not be obvious from the painting, but the question
then would be what had the color of Madame Matisse's dress to
do with how the artist painted it? Mallarmé's wonderful direc-
tive—*Peindre non la chose mais l'effet qu'elle produit*—might have
come to Matisse's lips at that point, but *then* the question would
be: What is meant by "the effect"? We know that Amalie Matisse
was a strong and determined woman, who supported her family as
a milliner at a time when Matisse was selling almost nothing. The
spectacular hat is the chief element in the painting, and I like to
believe Matisse showed her wearing that hat for reasons like those
that moved Pope Julius to ask Michelangelo to depict him with a
sword—that hat was her sword, the emblem of her victory, her

FIGURE 12   Henri Matisse, *Woman with Hat*, 1905
A moral advertisement

dignity, and her force. It was a moral advertisement: in 1905, a woman wearing a hat like that could face the world and take on all comers. *Of course* she would be wearing black! And Matisse himself had to make his portrait as brave and powerful as his wife by taking great risks with form and with color. Roger Fry misses this entirely by saying that Matisse was interested in design and that the design is what we should be looking at and would in time find beautiful—that the artist distorts is in the interests of design. No: in my view at least it is a strong painting of a strong woman. But it is not a beautiful painting of a beautiful woman. And in truth there is no way, without doing violence to the concept, to see the painting as beautiful. One's initial impression of it as ugly is closer to the artistic truth it expresses. But of course to grasp the truth one does have to stop seeing it as ugly because of the way it was drawn. The "bad" drawing was part of "the effect."

When one executes a piece of art criticism such as this, it is inevitable that someone will say that she or he really sees *Woman with a Hat* as beautiful. When, in a conference on beauty some years ago, I mentioned Matisse's *Blue Nude* as a painting that could not be seen as beautiful, a fellow art critic disagreed by saying that *he* saw it as beautiful. *Blue Nude* was one of the scandals of the 1913 Armory Show, the other being Duchamp's *Nude Descending a Staircase*. The scandal of the latter was that no one could find the nude. It seemed that viewers were told one thing and shown another—that they could not trust their eyes. Even Duchamp's fellow cubists had problems with his painting, and asked that he withdraw it from an exhibition in Paris. Perhaps it was because he sought to depict movement, in violation of some convention regarding stasis in cubist art. The case of *Blue Nude* was somewhat different: if someone were to have asked Matisse what was the color of his model's skin, he might have replied impatiently "Obviously pink." The blue was in the painting, which violated the principle of transparency. What could Matisse have been getting at? Why paint as blue what in reality is pink? And why paint as hideous what might in reality have been beautiful—or at least pretty? When one says that *Blue Nude* is beautiful, one is merely expressing admiration for its strength and power, for Matisse's decision to present us with a powerful painting rather than a pleasing one, to draw our attention to the painting rather than to the person—or to express, by hypotyposis, the power of female beauty through the power of a painting that is not beautiful at all. Most of the world's art is not beautiful, nor was the production of beauty part of its purpose. *Blue Nude* is morally rather than visually true. Beauty is really as obvious as blue: one does not have to work at seeing it when it is there. One has rather to work at seeing a painting as good despite its not being beautiful, when one had been supposing that beauty was the way artistic goodness was to be understood.

I want one further example, which comes from Hegel, a great art critic, writing about a masterpiece by the artist the Pre-Raphaelites were to despise. "It is a familiar and frequently repeated critical reproach against Raphael's *Transfiguration* that it falls apart into two actions entirely devoid of any connection with one another," Hegel writes. "And in fact this is true if this picture is considered externally: above on the hill we see the transfiguration, below is the scene with the child possessed of an unclean spirit.

> But if we look at the *spirit* of the composition, a supreme connection is not to be missed. For, on the one hand, Christ's visible transfiguration is precisely his elevation above the earth, and his departure from his disciples, and this must be made visible too as a separation and a departure; on the other hand, the sublimity of Christ is here especially transfigured in an actual simple case, namely in the fact that the Disciples could not help the child without the help of the Lord. Thus here the double action is motivated throughout and the connection is displayed within and without in the fact that one disciple expressly points to Christ who has departed from them and thereby he hints at the true destiny of the Son of God to be at the same time on earth, so that the saying will be true: Where two or three are gathered in my name, there am I in the midst of them.

"Design" is as weak as "beauty" is inappropriate in responding to this tremendous work. The design is entailed by the meaning Raphael means to convey—*l'effet* of the event he has undertaken to depict by visual means when the meaning of transfiguration is not entirely visual. Ruskin would be right about Raphael: "externally" *The Transfiguration* lacks visual truth, but internally it conveys truth of a profounder kind. What we see in the painting could not have been seen by anyone there: they would either have been dazzled by Christ's transfiguration, or caught up with concern for the possessed child. Raphael brought these disparate perceptions together in a single astonishing vision.

One sees from this passage the remarkable difference between a thinker like Hegel, who was deeply engaged by great art, and

FIGURE 13   Raphael, *The Transfiguration*, 1518–1520
Disconnected by design

Kant, who was not, and for whom experiencing art was of a piece with experiencing natural beauty, like that of flowers or sunsets or lovely women. And this is finally what is missing in Moore's way of thinking of art as well. He thought of artistic beauty on the model of natural beauty, as we can see from his thought of how much better it would be for something beautiful to exist in reality than merely in pictures. He was not wrong in thinking that, when a painting was beautiful, it was beautiful in the way in which nature is beautiful. He was wrong in thinking that if a painting was good, it was because of its beauty, and that if he could not see the beauty, he would have to look harder, as his disciple Roger Fry insisted is required when we are dealing with difficult art.

David Hume, for all his astuteness, makes the same mistake, by thinking that there are two species of beauty. He takes this up almost as an aside, in order to point up an analogy between two views of moral truths, namely "whether they be derived from Reason or Sentiment." Sentimentalists claim that "To virtue it belongs to be *amiable*, and vice *odious*." The latter term evokes a distant echo to disgust: a moral revulsion that verges on physical recoil. By symmetry, the former evokes a kind of natural attraction: we are drawn to what we perceive as good in others. Hume allows that there is a kind of beauty of which the latter may be true: "Some species of beauty, especially the natural kinds, on their first appearance command our affection and approbation; and where they fail of this effect, it is impossible for any reasoning to redress their influence, or adapt them better to our taste and sentiment." It is in regard to this sort of beauty that one might say there is no disputing taste. But Hume, as a man of letters, had a vivid sense of the transformative power of critical reasoning. And here I repeat a great passage from his writing: "In many orders of beauty, particularly those of the finer arts, it is requisite to employ much reasoning in order to feel the proper sentiment; and a false relish may frequently be corrected by argument and reflection. There are just grounds to conclude that moral beauty partakes much of this latter species, and demands the assistance of our intellectual faculties in order to give it a suitable influence on the human mind."

The kind of reasoning Hume appeals to, I think, is illustrated in Hegel on Raphael's *Transfiguration*, or in that I sought to employ in discussing *Woman with a Hat* or *Blue Nude*. Hume was a man of letters, and his writing on literature gives evidence of the way in which we bring one another round to the point of seeing that one piece of writing is artistically better than another, and why it is so. His mistake lies in supposing that we are brought round by reasoning to apprehend its *beauty,* when what he really means is literary excellence, superiority, and depth. The term "aesthetic" was not in wide use in Hume's time, or at least not in English usage. It would have helped immensely had Hume been able to distinguish between *aesthetic* beauty and what we might call artistic beauty. It is aesthetic beauty that is discerned through the senses. Artistic beauty requires discernment and critical intelligence. *But why use the word beauty at all in this latter case?* Some people are beautiful, some are not, some are downright ugly. These are differences we register through the senses. We are attracted to people because of their beauty, and even fall in love with them because they are beautiful. But human beings have qualities of intellect and character that attract us to them despite their lack of beauty. When Alcibiades praises Socrates in the *Symposium,* he means to say that there are qualities in Socrates that engage him, and which override his conspicuous and legendary ugliness. Simone de Beauvoir loved Sartre not because he was beautiful but because of that unlikely constellation of intellectual and sexual qualities that made him Sartre. To be sure, we often commend these qualities by speaking of them as "beautiful"—but this has nothing to do with aesthetic considerations at all, and it seems to me that it muddles the concept of beauty irreparably if we say that these qualities are another species or order of beauty. It muddles it the way Paul McCarthy's enthusiasts do when they seek to find beauty in his overtly and undeniably disgusting work—"Not standard beauty, but the beauty of commitment and absorption." Comparably, we may come to admire Matisse's *Blue Nude,* despite its ugliness, above Chabanel's *Birth of Venus,* despite its transparent presentation of the goddess's pink beauty. I propose we restrict the concept of beauty to its aesthetic identity, which refers to the senses, and recognize in art something that in its highest instances belongs to thought. Where Fry, for all his artistic aventurousness went wrong was to insist that the Grafton paintings were beautiful when everyone who entered the gallery could see with their own eyes that they were not. Instead of that he developed his idea of the deferred beauty that rewards "hard looking." As though we would ultimately be rewarded by the kind of sensuous thrill that beauty in aesthetic sense causes in us without benefit of argument or analysis.

Hegel and the End of Art

Hegel is greatly to be admired because he is the first philosopher who attempts systematically to distinguish, perhaps too sharply, between aesthetics and the philosophy of art. Aesthetics, he observes, is "the science of sensation or feeling," and concerns art "when works of art are treated with regard to the feelings they were supposed to produce, as, for instance, the feeling of pleasure, admiration, fear, pity, and so on." This is a great advance over Kant, who more or less confines the relevant repertoire of affects to pleasure and pain, making an important exception for sublimity. Artistic beauty, Hegel insists is "higher" than the beauty of nature, and he wrote with a marvelous thunder that "The beauty of art is beauty *born of the spirit and born again*. What Hegel wanted to stress is that art is an *intellectual* product, and that its beauty too must express the thought the art embodies. But then why does he not argue that fear and pity, to take two examples that he assigns to aesthetics, are also intellectual products? They were deeply related to tragedy, according to Aristotle in the *Poetics,* and are components in catharsis, which is enlisted as part of the reason we relate to tragic presentations. He does not, evidently, because these are feelings, as the sense of beauty is as well when art is considered aesthetically. But what exactly then is *artistic* beauty when it is not aesthetic?

It is here, I think, that Hegel becomes confused and probably inconsistent, for he writes that "the beauty of art presents itself to *sense*, feeling, intuition, imagination; it has a different sphere than thought, and the apprehension of its activity and its products demands an organ other than scientific thinking." That is why in large part art has come to an end, to invoke his celebrated thesis. We have risen above the sphere of sense in the respect that *philosophy*—or *Wissenschaft*—is an exercise of pure understanding and analysis. What he prizes art for is that in its various golden ages, it did what philosophy can do, but in a limited way because of the constraint of sensuous media: "The beautiful days of Greek art, like the golden age of the later Middle Ages are gone." By contrast with the experience of art "The development of reflection in our life today has made it a need of ours . . . to cling to general considerations and to regulate the particular by them, with the result that the universal forms, laws, duties, rights, maxims, prevail as determining reasons and are the chief regulator." With art "we demand . . . a quality of life in which the universal is not present in the form of law and maxim, but which gives the impression of being one with the senses and the feelings." So "the conditions of our present time are not favorable to art." The end of art in Hegel thus has nothing to do with the decline of art but with the fact that we no longer require that ideas be communicated in sensuous form. So art could be glorious and it would still be over, as far as Hegel is concerned. In a way, his object to art is something like Kant's objection to the use of examples. Examples are, as Kant puts it, "the go-cart of the understanding." For Hegel, art was the go-cart of spirit. We enter the highest stage of what he calls Absolute Spirit when we no longer require art to satisfy our "highest needs."

But this leaves us with the question of how beauty, understood in sensuous terms, can really be "born of the spirit and born again." Hegel does not give us good examples of artistic beauty. He gives us good examples of art, the excellence of which can be brought out through astute art criticism, as in his magnificent account of the *Transfiguration,* or in his unmatched analysis of Dutch paintings, which really are, or often are, beautiful—but beautiful in a sensuous way. No one admires Hegel's philosophy of art more than I. What we must do in order to accept it is to recognize the way art can, indeed must, be rational and sensuous at once. And then determine how its sensuous properties are related to its rational content, which will be my task for the remainder of this book.

Duchamp and Art Without Aesthetics

Consider once again Marcel Duchamp, whose art neither Hegel nor any of his contemporaries could have considered as such. It was Duchamp above all others whose work was intended to exemplify the most radical dissociation of aesthetics from art, particularly in his readymades of 1915–1917. In 1924, Duchamp made it clear that finding an object with no aesthetic qualities was far from simple, but we can get a sense for his intention if we consider his

Comb (1916), which Calvin Tompkins characterizes "the most serenely anaesthetic of all Duchamp's readymades." No one can be said to have either good or bad taste in metal grooming combs! They embody the principle of the readymade through the fact that there is "no beauty, no ugliness, nothing particularly aesthetic about it," and from this perspective one of them is as good as any other. But he certainly never liberated his art from what we might term objecthood, nor hence from sensation. At a symposium held at the Museum of Modern Art in 1961, Duchamp spoke on the relationship between the readymades and "Art"—understood to mean the aesthetically pleasing. He said that he did not see the readymades as "coming to nothingness or zero" but that he was doing something "without having to invoke aestheticism or feeling or taste or any of these elements." And he concluded "I don't want to destroy art for anybody else but myself." What then if an artist means to reintroduce beauty, that being after all an option, if not for Duchamp then for others?

Duchamp gave a kind of answer to this in connection with his most notorious readymade, the urinal he attempted to get accepted under the title *Fountain* in the 1917 Society of Independent Artists' exhibition. As is well known, the work was signed R. Mutt—not known at the time to be one of Duchamp's myriad aliases. After the fiasco, he wrote "The Richard Mutt Case" in the short-lived magazine, *The Blind Man,* saying that "Mr. Mutt . . . took an ordinary article of life, placed it so that its useful significance disappeared under the new title and point of view—created a new thought for that object." Identifying this "new thought" has obsessed his interpreters since 1917. Duchamp's patron, Walter Arensburg, supposed that the thought was "A lovely form has been revealed." That, I think, is inconsistent with the philosophy of the readymade, but I have no wish to press the matter here. The point is that the work is the thought plus the object, it being in part a function of the thought to determine which properties of the *object* belong to the *work*. The urinal may be beautiful—and an argument could be made that as a piece of domestic furnishing it was intended to be attractive and express the very substance of sanitary purity in its glazed whiteness. But was beauty relevant to Mr. Mutt's thought? The object may be beautiful, but not necessarily the *work*. We have to identify the meaning of the work as given by the thought, in order to see whether the work is beautiful. And this would be the way Hume would enjoin us to see the matter. It is "our intellectual faculties" that identify the thought through which the object is to be interpreted. And our intellectual faculties direct us to those of its sensuous qualities which bear upon its interpretation. Was the beauty of the urinal relevant to the goodness of *Fountain?* Or is it merely relevant to the goodness of urinals relative to the principles that govern the interior decoration of bathrooms, without having anything to do with the "thought" of *Fountain* itself? Or better, does the beauty, if indeed there is beauty, contribute or not to the *meaning* of the work?

These are matters that cannot be determined without reference to an interpretation of *Fountain.* Jean Clair writes that the symbolic role of the urinal "is not to raise the status of a manufactured object to that of a work of art [but] to underwrite the archaic sacralization of human refuse and the infantile worship on one's own dung." It is for this reason that he explains the aesthetics of disgust above all through the influence of Duchamp. I by contrast see Duchamp as the artist who above all has sought to produce an art without aesthetics, and to replace the sensuous with the intellectual, as Hegel insisted has been achieved as a matter of course by the historical evolution of the "spirit." As I see it, the aesthetics of the urinal, as a plumbing fixture, has no role in its meaning. Neither has it any meaning in Jean's Clair interpretation, since it is its association with disgust that inflects its historical importance. It is too controversial a case to use to show how beauty and meaning are internally connected when the beauty of a work *is* part of its identity.

The Apple Trees at Balbec

I want now to present a pair of examples, one of natural, one of artistic beauty, in both of which beauty plays a pivotal role in experience. The beauty in both cases is aesthetic. And it is, moreover, simple and striking, in the sense that it would present itself to anyone as such, without benefit of much by way of education. In the artistic case, however, there may be *resistance* to the beauty because of certain prejudices regarding art. In order to accept the beauty, these resistances have to be overcome by a kind of education in what art is. This education does not lead to some higher order of beauty, because there is no higher order. What it leads to is an understanding of how aesthetic beauty plays a role in the meaning of the work to which it belongs. One can say that in such a case, the beauty is born of the spirit because the meaning of the work is internally related to its aesthetic qualities. The beauty is part of the experience of the art. But the experience is richer by far than the "retinal shudder" Duchamp impugned, not because it is something to be ashamed of, but because there is more to art than optical thrills.

I have selected the examples because they raise some striking psychological issues which bear on the moral grounds evoked in treating beauty as shallow and false to the reality of the world. I intend the examples, in brief, to help remove the stigma from beauty, to restore to beauty some of what gave it the moral weight it had in Edwardian aesthetics. Needless to say, it is not my purpose to plead for beauty's restoration to the definition or essence of art!

The first, somewhat overdetermined example comes from Proust. In a section called "The Intermitancies of the Heart," in the fourth volume of *In Search of Lost Time,* the Narrator has returned to the seaside resort of Balbec. On his first stay there, he had been accompanied by his beloved grandmother, who has since died. The section of the book in which he describes his grandmother's death is curiously clinical and detached, which is somewhat inconsistent with what we would expect, given their earlier bond: we feel we have learned something through this about the character of Marcel, who seems a much colder person than we would have believed him to be. This proves to be false: the moment he sits in his room at the Grand Hotel, he is overwhelmed with a sense of loss and bereavement, and descends into an acute depression in which his grandmother's irrevocable absence floods his consciousness completely. Marcel now sits gazing at his grandmother's photograph, which tortures him. He realizes how self-centered he had been when he had been the object of his grandmother's totally dedicated love—how he had failed, for example, to notice how ill she had been on that first sojourn to Balbec. This mood lasts until he goes for a walk one day in the direction of a high road, along which he and his grandmother used to be driven in the carriage of Mme. de Villeparisis. The road was muddy, which made him think of his grandmother and how she used to return covered with mud when she went walking, whatever the weather. The sun is out, and he sees a "dazzling spectacle" which consists of a stand of apple trees in blossom.

> The disposition of the apple trees, as far as the eye could reach, . . . in full bloom, unbelievably luxuriant, their feet in the mire beneath their ball-dresses, heedless of spoiling the most marvelous pink satin that was ever seen, which glittered in the sunlight; the distant horizon of the sea gave the trees the background of a Japanese print; If I raised my head to gaze at the sky through the flowers, which made its serene blue appear almost violent, they seemed to draw apart to reveal the immensity of their paradise. Beneath that azure a faint but cold breeze set the blushing bouquets. [It was] as though it had been an amateur of exotic art and colors that had artificially created this living beauty. But it moved one to tears because, to whatever lengths it went in its effects of refined artifice, one felt that it was natural, that these apple trees were there in the heart of the country.

The example is overdetermined because only someone like Marcel would have seen this glorious sight as he did. He is like his counterpart, Swann, in seeing everything through the metaphors of art. Someone who had never seen prints by Hiroshige or an Ascension of the Virgin, or in whose life there were no ball-gowns, or pink satin, could hardly have experienced the apple trees quite as he did. Still, it was a piece of natural beauty, which might have taken the breath away from anyone fortunate enough to have seen it. Marcel tells us that from this moment, his grief for his grandmother began to diminish: metaphorically, one might say, she had entered paradise.

The apple trees at Balbec might be on anyone's short list for G.E. Moore's world of beauty. A world with such sights in it would be better, Moore is confident in arguing, than a world of ashes. That would be as obvious as the fact that his two hands exist, to invoke one of Moore's most famous arguments. You cannot argue anyone into accepting that if they are uncertain of it—for what could be more certain than it, on which a proof could be based? If they doubt that, their doubt is irremediable. This I think is Hume's point about natural beauty. You can't argue anyone into feeling it. The natural beauty was at the core of Marcel's experience, even if there was an aura of metaphors drawn from his experience of art, which enters into his descriptions. One could be uplifted by the beauty of the apple-trees without bringing to the experience the needs that they helped Marcel resolve. But the example involves beauty as an ingredient in healing a sickness of the heart. The Prophet Isaiah writes:

> *Give unto them beauty for ashes,*
> *the oil of joy for mourning, the*
> *garment of praise for the spirit of heaviness.*

Marcel had been given beauty for ashes.

The Vietnam Memorial

My second example is of a relatively contemporary work, Maya Lin's *Vietnam Veterans' Memorial* of 1982, which I select because it is widely regarded as possessing great beauty, both by those in the art world and by quite ordinary persons for whom it has become one of the most widely admired sights in Washington, D.C. The Memorial is simplicity itself. It consists of two symmetrical triangular wings, sharing a vertical base, and bent away from one another at a mild angle—125 degrees—like arms, one might say, which gently enfold those who approach it. It is a very reduced form of the structure in front of St. Peter's in Rome, but performing the same role. Maya Lin was an undergraduate at Yale when she presented the idea, and was told by her instructor that the angle between the two wings "had to mean something." The two walls are in polished black granite, and inscribed with the names of every American soldier killed in the Vietnam War, about 58,000 in all, listed in chronological order rather than, as somewhere along the line had been suggested, in alphabetical order. Lin's fellow students criticized the work as "visual poetry"—it is, after all, a kind of book—but were uncertain of its architectural merit. It took her all of six weeks to complete the winning model, selected unanimously from 1,421 entries in blind review. It has the quality of a fairy tale: Maya Ying Lin was twenty-one years old, of Oriental descent, and had lost no one she loved in the conflict. She failed all the tacit tests the designer of such a memorial was supposed to meet. The jurors naturally supposed it was by a man.

When the organizer of the competition, a rifleman in the Vietnam struggle, Jan Scruggs, first saw the work he was profoundly disillusioned. "A big bat. A weird-looking thing that could have been from Mars. Maybe a third-grader had entered the competition. All the fund's work had gone into making a huge bat for veterans. Maybe it symbolized a boomerang." Scruggs thought, "It's weird and I wish I knew what the hell it is." It is amazing that it was not voted down. Everyone wondered how the general public would react, but one person told Scruggs that "You would be surprised how sophisticated the general public really is." That of course turned out to be true. But the structure of controversy was at first governed by the fact that people held views to the effect that a memorial should not be "abstract." That explains why, to placate them, the sculpture of a trio of highly realistic soldiers was erected in front of the memorial. By 1982, however, the general public had benefited by having traveled and visited museums, and having studied art history in school, or simply from having seen programs about art on television. It was prepared to accept beauty that moved it. In 1982, Tony Silvers and Henry Chalfont made a film, *Style Wars*, about the graffiti then being painted on the sides of subway cars in New York. The "writers," as they called themselves, were from the poor sectors of society—from housing projects and often from broken families. But they had a remarkable sophistication and artistic literacy, as one can tell from the iconography of their works.

The beauty of the *Memorial* is almost instantly felt, and then perhaps analyzed and explained by reference to the way the visitors, many of whom come to see the name of someone they knew or loved, and to do a rubbing of it to carry home, see themselves reflected in the same wall that carries the name of the dead, as if there were a community of the living and the dead, though death itself is forever. It is possible to see the three soldiers reflected in the wall, and one can even read them as seeing themselves reflected there, as well as in having their names inscribed in the Book of the Dead. If one is sympathetic, one can even see the memorial as a vision that appears to them, explaining their rapt expressions. Possibly there is an analogy to a natural phenomenon, the surface of a very still body of water in which the sky is reflected, as in Monet's immense paintings of water-lilies, which is my model for thinking about the Wall, since those paintings make visible the way clouds and flowers seem to occupy the same space. Whatever the explanation of the felt beauty of the Wall, it is understood with reference to the "thought." It is part of the meaning of the work. In Proust's orchard, the thought is his. In the *Vietnam Veteran's Memorial*, the thought belongs to the work and explains the beauty. In natural beauty, the beauty is external to the thought, in art the beauty is internal to the work.

Jan Scruggs's account of how the memorial came into being is titled *To Heal a Nation*. It was his idea that the terrible political wounds caused by the war could only be healed by a memorial erected in the Mall in Washington, D.C., which is in effect sacred soil. To the extent that a work of art is capable of healing a nation, the *Vietnam Veterans' Memorial* is in candidacy for such an achievement. But I predict that it will be seen as beautiful, and its beauty seen as internal to its meaning, well after the conflict that gave rise to it fades in the national memory—the way the War of 1812 has, for example. Like the apple trees of Balbec, it may lift the spirits without necessarily healing the soul.

Internal Beauty

I certainly have no wish to build the idea of healing into the analysis of beauty as such, since we are not always ailing when we are struck by the beauty of something. Sometimes beauty simply stops us in our tracks. "My heart leaps up when I behold a rainbow in the sky" expresses a core perception of beauty, the poetry coming after the beholding takes place. "Earth has not anything to show more fair" was avowedly written from the roof of a coach bound for France: "This city now doth like a garment wear/The beauty of the morning" We have all had those aesthetic surprises. And we have them even in museums.

I remember first seeing one of Robert Motherwell's *Elegies for the Spanish Republic* while walking through an exhibition of abstract painting at the Metropolitan Museum, knowing nothing about it or about him at the time, but knowing, immediately and intuitively, that it was something I had to stop for. At the time, I made no effort to analyze the work critically, but, I shall show in Chapter 5 how Motherwell's *Elegies* were to become a paradigm for me in thinking about the place of beauty in the philosophy of art.

What interests me at this point is, however, the idea of "internal beauty," where the beauty of the object is internal to the meaning of the work. It is connected to the "thought" of the Vietnam Memorial that it be experienced as beautiful. By contrast, on at least my reading of *Fountain,* the beauty of the urinal is external to Mr. Mutt's thought, which we must attempt to recover in order to experience the work as we ought. Natural beauty is perhaps always external, unless we see the world itself as a work of art, and its meaning the symbol of its goodness. Something like this would have been Kant's view, which ascribed far greater importance to natural than to artistic beauty, so far as there were grounds for distinguishing them. He saw in natural beauty the assurance of a deep intended harmony between the world and us.

Internal beauty requires no such metaphysical assumptions. It serves to illustrate one mode in which feeling is connected with the thoughts that animate works of art. There are modes other than beauty, of course, that connect feeling and thought in works of art: disgust, eroticism, sublimity, as well as pity and fear and the other cases Hegel mentions as having to do with aesthetics. And these modes help explain why art is important in human life, despite Hegel's brash claim that we have reached a stage in the history of spirit when philosophy alone can satisfy "the deepest interests of mankind and the most comprehensive truths of the spirit." Because these interests are connected with the way we are made, they might help us begin the detoxification of beauty in contemporary art and philosophy, always recognizing that both have shown that it is not part of the definition of art. Beauty may be a mode among the many modes through which thoughts are presented to human sensibility, and explain the relevance of art to human existence, and why room for them must be found in an adequate definition of art.

5

Beauty and Politics

When Dave Hickey floated the idea, in 1993, that beauty would be the defining problem of the decade, it would have been difficult to find much by way of corroboration for such a forecast in the art being made at that time. The work presented in the 1993 Whitney Biennial, for example, was for the most part accusatory, and angrily political in character. Visitors were polarized at the admissions desk, where they were issued flat metal badges, designed by Daniel Martinez and themselves one of the artworks included in the show, which bore all or part of the provocative slogan "I can't imagine ever wanting to be white." Also part of the show was the famous videotape, played continuously, showing over and over the beating of Rodney King by members of the LAPD. The person who had made the tape was not an artist, but

FIGURE 14 Daniel Martinez, *Admission Badges*, 1993
Polarizing slogans

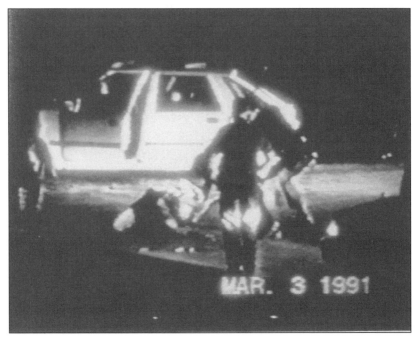

FIGURE 14   George Holliday's videotape of the Rodney King beating,
             1991
             Not the work of an artist

simply someone who happened to be there with a camcorder, and
there were questions raised as to whether it ought to have been
included at all, since its status as a work of art was uncertain. It had
not been submitted, in the manner of Duchamp's *Fountain* in
1917, but had, rather, been selected by the curators of the show,
who decided what was to be exhibited and what was not, and its
presence reflected the changing status of curators, who were
increasingly becoming the defining figures of the art world. More
and more members of the 1990s curatoriat had come of age in the
1960s, and saw art as a means of advancing political and social
agendas. But at the moment the distinction between art and visual
culture was under pressure, and the tape certainly reflected what
had happened to the definition of art in the sixties, when so much
that had long been thought to form part of the concept of art had
been eliminated. Who said that to be a work of art something had
to be made by an artist? It was in any case clear that nothing made
by an artist, least of all by a video artist, had anything like the

impact on society that the King tape had had. Aired nationally and internationally on television, it became an emblem of the strained relationships between minorities and the police in American cities. It became an agency of change. Whether it was art mattered less to the curators than the kind of reality it showed. In that respect it stood as a model for a politically committed art. It had helped transform society.

The 1993 Biennial was deeply resented. It was resented in large measure because in attempting to transform society, its immediate effect was to transform the museum as an institution that was still thought of in terms that Henry James would have understood, as an institution dedicated to knowledge, if not indeed as a sanctuary for beauty. James's great character in his late novel, *The Golden Bowl*, the art collector Adam Verver, had himself been transformed by beauty, and was dedicating himself to a life of aesthetic philanthropy. His vision was to bestow on American City a museum filled with objects of beauty for the benefit of its aesthetically deprived citizenry. His aim was to make accessible to them a kind of knowledge ordinarily available only to persons of cultivated leisure, with time and money enough to experience works of artistic beauty in the conviction that this was one of life's supreme goods. This exalted view of art had undergone a great many changes since the abuse of beauty by the Intractable Avant-Garde, which began only a decade after the novel's publication, but the museum was still thought of as a place of knowledge. Art retained a certain aura of sanctity, though the knowledge that museums purveyed was increasingly the knowledge of art itself. It would, I think, be extremely ill-advised for a museum in quest of funds today to justify its solicitations on grounds that Verver took for granted. If they are not aesthetic skeptics, funding agents are disposed to think of beauty as a luxury rather than a spiritual necessity. Public funding is predicated on education, but what have museums to put in place of poor battered Beauty today?

Two educational models have evolved in museums in recent decades—the art-appreciation model, and the cultural insight model. In the latter the art is a means to knowledge of a culture; in the former art is an object of knowledge in its own right. It is knowledge of art as art, and this often means arriving at an understanding of works through noting their formal features. This may or may not be accompanied by historical explanations—what work

influenced the artist, and perhaps what work the artist herself influenced. Still, the object of knowledge is the artwork, and funding
agencies might wonder what is the value of such knowledge, and
they might, again, raise the issue of elitism. Is it justified to spend
the taxpayer's money on something so unconnected with the lives
of those who tramp through the museums, let alone the lives of
those who don't? If one responds by saying that knowing about art
does something the taxpayers *should* think is valuable, well, it
would be valuable to say what it is. And it is here that the other
model is brought forward. Art helps us understand the cultures to
which it belongs, and in the particular case of American art, it helps
Americans understand their own culture and hence themselves.
Much of the Whitney's advertising promises that its shows will
help viewers "make sense" of America. Works of art are so many
windows into the inner life of the culture—and of ourselves as
members of the culture.

And this would have been seen as the function of the Whitney
Biennials. They are intended to provide knowledge of what
American artists have been doing in the preceding two years. Those
who attended Biennial 1993 expected to gain knowledge. And in a
sense this *is* what they gained: they learned that American artists
were deeply engaged in opposing the injustices of race, of class, of
gender in America. But the artists were not simply concerned that
the viewers should know what they were doing. Those viewers were
themselves part of the society the artists were concerned to change.
The problems were their problems too. The implication is that you
are not just to look at what we, the artists, have done: you have to
help us change the world. The show itself was like the admissions
badges: you were somehow engaged in issues of race in the act of
attaching them to your jacket lapel. The visitors were put on the
spot. And this is not what they had come for; this is not what they
expected to happen to them in the museum, this is not what they
wanted the museum to be or art to be.

Good Art Can Be Ugly

It can be seen in hindsight that the 1993 Biennial was a high-water
mark of the politically tumultuous 1980s. And perhaps Hickey saw
more deeply than those who were caught up in the ideological
conflicts being enacted in the art world of those years that a

period—or at least a phase of art history—was nearing an end. In that case Hickey's conjecture might have been that artistic activism had run its course, and that a return to beauty might be a natural reflex. In that same extraordinary year, 1993, the art history department of the University of Texas in Austin sponsored a conference devoted to the question "Whatever Happened to Beauty?" Its organizer, the distinguished art historian Richard Schiff, posed the question in terms of whether the pursuit of what he called "artistic excellence" was compatible with "socio-economic discourse."

I find it interesting that he should have used the expression "artistic excellence" as more or less synonymous with "beauty." But it is extremely important to distinguish between *aesthetic* beauty and a wider sense of artistic excellence where aesthetic beauty may not be relevant at all. Let us once again consider Roger Fry's crucial discussion of the Post-Impressionist painting he showed early in the last century in London, which critics found so appalling. Fry was unquestionably right to defend the works as artistically excellent, but wrong to say that they would be seen as beautiful when one came to understand the principles on which they were made. His critics entered his exhibitions with a certain fixed idea of what a painting should look like, and what they saw was so dissonant with that that they could hardly regard it as art. Modernism had changed what paintings were going to look like. But Fry made it sound as if they were going to look aesthetically beautiful once they were understood. And my thought has been that it is important to recognize that the works might still be perceived as ugly even when we have come to see their "artistic excellence." The recognition of excellence need not entail a transformation in aesthetic perception. They don't change before ones eyes, like frogs into princes. That is my argument regarding such modernist works as Matisse's *Woman with a Hat* and *Blue Nude*. The ugly does not become beautiful just because the ugly art is good. My sense is that artistic excellence is connected with what the art is supposed to do, what effect it is intended to have. The work in Biennial 1993 was intended to change the way we think and act on matters of injustice. A feminist work is not intended to secure our admiration for itself, but to compel a change in the way women are thought about and treated in our society. If it has that effect, if it makes viewers see injustices where before they were blind or indifferent to them, it is artistically excellent. One may study the work from the perspective of how it achieved its intended effect. But that is not the primary way in which we are meant to relate to it. The work is meant to change the way those who view it view the world. To see the world as a scene of injustice is *ipso facto* to be moved to change it.

In any case, most of those who spoke at "Whatever Happened to Beauty?" took the term "artistic excellence" to mean aesthetic beauty—work that was artistically excellent *because* it was aesthetically beautiful—and their response, especially so with the artists, was that beauty was alive and well in *their* work. And so it was—but that left unaddressed the question of whether there is a conflict between beauty and "socio-economic discourse." I would now like to rephrase Schiff's question: Can art be aesthetically beautiful when its content concerns social issues? In the 1993 Biennial, for example, Sue Williams presented an installation that concerns the victimization of women. It included a fairly realistic pool of (plastic) vomit, an obvious enough elicitor of disgust. And it almost certainly expressed the artist's revulsion toward men as sexual oppressors. Would it be a valid criticism of the work that it lacked aesthetic beauty? Or, conversely, would it have been a valid criticism of a work that addressed the same subject and expressed the same attitude, that it was beautiful? Is there or is there not an internal conflict between beauty and certain contents? Or better: is not disgust the more appropriate aesthetic for an art that deals with the kind of content advanced in Sue Williams's piece? Was it a mark of "artistic excellence" that her piece should have aroused disgust in her viewers—not so much with the work but with what the work was about? So that beauty in connection with that content would not be irrelevant but artistically wrong?

Motherwell's *Elegies*

Let's consider a case where aesthetic beauty is artistically right—Robert Motherwell's *Elegies for the Spanish Republic*. I have already mentioned how beautiful I found one of these paintings to be when I first saw it, without knowing anything more about it than that. The critic Clement Greenberg used to cover his eyes while someone put a painting in place, and then abruptly opened them, acting on the thesis that what strikes the eye without refer-

FIGURE 16   Robert Motherwell, *Elegy for the Spanish Republic No. 172 (with Blood)*, 1989 © Dedalus Foundation, Inc./Licensed by VAGA, New York, NY
The beauty belongs to the meaning.

ence to previous thought is the test of a painting's excellence. In a way, Greenberg's methodology connects with a thought on beauty by Kant. Kant writes that "The beautiful is that which apart from concepts is represented as the object of universal satisfaction." I want to stress "apart from concepts." It suggests that beauty is a non-conceptual content of certain experiences, which of course can contribute to a larger experience of an artwork, when it is taken up as part of the latter's meaning, as we saw in the previous chapter. Greenberg, if I am right, sought to get an impression of the object before a concept could come into play, and rest his judgment of the work on this conceptually uncontaminated "first glimpse." In my own view, we have no clear idea of how much extra-aesthetic information comes with the first glimpse. But I must admit that when I first saw Motherwell's painting, I knew that it was beautiful by this test—I had been stopped in my tracks by its beauty. At the time I did not much reflect on what it meant. But when I did, I came to the view that the *Elegies*—Motherwell painted over 170 of them by the time of his death—

were artistically excellent not simply because they were beautiful but because their being beautiful was artistically right. By that I mean that when I grasped their *thought*, I understood that their aesthetic beauty was internal to their meaning.

The *Elegies* are characteristically large black-and-white compositions, with occasionally a spot of red or ochre. There are usually two or three black ovals interspersed with wide vertical bars. They are freely and rather urgently painted—the black paint feels as if it is splashed on, with some residual spatters and drips. *Elegy for the Spanish Republic 172 (with Blood)* also has a *tache* of blood-red paint. Viewers have read the forms in different ways. Some have seen the ovals as the testicles, the uprights as the penis of a bull, but this loses plausibility when there are more than two ovals and more than one vertical. Some see ovals and uprights with reference to the traditional egg-and-dart decorative motif, but that makes the title of the paintings obscure. I saw the ovals as figures in black shawls, and the verticals as broken uprights, as if remnants of shattered buildings. The beauty of the paintings does not translate into thinking that what these forms represent are themselves beautiful. "How beautiful those mourning women are beside the shattered posts of their burned and bombed houses, standing against the pale morning sky" is not a morally permissible vision. If, that is, one were to see a sight like that in reality and find it beautiful, one would wonder what sort of monster one had turned into, and quickly think instead of what could be done to help. Motherwell's stark black forms nevertheless do feel like shapeless figures set in a broken landscape, which has to be a scene of suffering. But the works are unquestionably beautiful as befits the mood announced by their titles as elegies. They are visual meditations on the death of a form of life. Elegies are part music and part poetry, whose language and cadence are constrained by the subject of death and loss and which express grief, whether the artist shares it or not. The *Spanish Elegies*, as they are called, express, in the most haunting forms and colors, rhythms and proportions, the death of a political ideal, whatever the awful realities that may historically have been part of it.

Elegy fits one of the great human moods; it is a way of responding artistically to what cannot be endured or what can only be endured. Motherwell was honored by the Spanish government, after the death of Franco, for having sustained the only mood morally acceptable through the years of dictatorship, a kind of abiding moral memory unmatched, I think, by anything else in twentieth-century art. Picasso's *Guernica,* for example, is not elegiac. It expresses shock and outrage. It too is black and white, but it would be false to call it beautiful. It was widely exhibited to raise money for anti-fascist causes. In its way, *Guernica* was painted in the spirit that inflected the work in Whitney Biennial 1993.

Elegies are artistic responses to events the natural *emotional* response to which is sorrow, which Webster's defines as "deep distress and regret (as over the loss of something loved)." I feel we understand too little about the psychology of loss to understand why the creation of beauty is so fitting as a way of marking it—why we bring flowers to the graveside, or to the funeral, or why music of a certain sort defines the mood of mourners. It is as though beauty works as a catalyst, transforming raw grief into a tranquil sadness, helping the tears to flow and, at the same time, one might say, putting the loss into a certain philosophical perspective. Recourse to beauty seems to emerge spontaneously on occasions where sorrow is felt. In the 1980s, when so many young men were beginning to die of AIDS, the gay funeral became a kind of art form. The victims would plan their funerals with care and originality, and fill them with what had given beauty to their lives. The beauty embodied the values they had lived by. Again, in the immediate aftermath of the terrorist attack on the World Trade Center, impromptu shrines appeared all over New York City. They were all more or less the same, and very moving: votive candles, flowers, flags, balloons, sometimes scraps of paper with poems. They were the immediate vernacular responses to the immense sadness that overcame everyone in New York. The mood was elegiac rather than angry, and the shrines were the outward expression of hearts broken by what was perceived as the end of a form of life. "Nothing will ever be the same" was the common remark in those first days after 9/11.

The conjunction of beauty with the occasion of moral pain somehow transforms the pain from grief into sorrow, and with that into a form of release. And since the occasion of the elegy is public, the sorrow is shared. It is no longer one's own. We are taken up into a community of mourners. The effect of the elegy is philosophical and artistic at once: it gives a kind of meaning to the loss by putting it at a distance, and by closing the distance between those who feel it—who are in it, as we say, together. I think this is what the Spanish government must have felt that Motherwell's paintings had done. They kept the feeling alive. Because these are elegies, they universalize through philosophization. But there is another kind of response, precisely the response of anger—the response evoked by *Guernica* in the case of art and "the war against terrorism" in the case of politics. It is one thing when distant empires have collapsed, and all that remain are the ruins, the trunkless legs of Ozymandias, King of Kings, and the boastful legend is rendered instantly pathetic by the surrounding wastes and the thin desert winds. We do sentimentalize ruins, which is why they were so stirring to the temperament of the Romantics, who could stand beneath or within them, and reflect on the transitoriness of glory. But we hardly can do this before raw wreckage, where the blackness is not so much the patination of age and nature, but the charred effect of fire and dried blood. Is the elegiac mood ever appropriate to so close a political catastrophe? Doesn't beauty distance it too abruptly? Have we a moral right to wax elegiac over something that was not all that inevitable or universal or necessary? Think, to bring it back to the individual death, to which beauty itself is the human response, when one feels that death was not inevitable (though death abstractly considered is): suppose one's lover has died of AIDS, and one feels that something should or could have been done, one feels anger that it has not been done, one blames and accuses: then beauty to which one is spontaneously moved also seems wrong, wrong because one is called upon to act (to "act up") and not to philosophize. Then elegy conflicts with the impulse to counteraction and the prolongation of struggle.

This might be a criticism to which Motherwell's paintings are subject. The *vita contemplative* and the *vita activa* point to different paths, in art no less than in moral conduct. My immediate concern is philosophical. It is to stress that the beauty of Motherwell's paintings is internal. The paintings are not to be admired because they are beautiful, but because their being so is internally connected with their reference and their mood. The beauty is ingredient in the content of the work, just as it is, in my view, with the cadences of sung or declaimed elegies. But it is also true that it is wrong at times to present as beautiful what calls, if not for action, then at least for indignation. Beauty is not always right. Sabastao

Salgado's photographs of suffering humanity are beautiful, as his work invariably is. But have we a right to show suffering of that order in beautiful ways? Doesn't the beauty of the representation imply that its content is somehow inevitable, like death? Are the photographs not unedifyingly dissonant, their beauty jarring with the painfulness of their content? If beauty is internally connected to the content of a work, it can be a criticism of a work that it is beautiful when it is inappropriate for it to be so.

Beauty As Consolation and As Relish

In a review of John Richardson's life of Picasso, the London critic, Richard Dorment, writes:

> It now seems odd that for one moment Picasso thought that Puvis de Chavannes's decorative classicism might be an adequate conduit for the tragic emotions he sought to express in the series of paintings inspired by the syphilitic prostitutes in the Saint-Lazare prison, but he did. Many of his gorgeously maudlin paintings of these lonely figures shuffling across empty landscapes or huddled in the white moonlight are fundamentally phony because their seductive beauty is at odds with the genuine misery on which they are based.

I am uncertain of this assessment, simply because I am uncertain of its implications for Motherwell's *Elegies*. What artistic address *is* appropriate to the depiction of jailed prostitutes? A clear documentary style conveys one message, a depiction embodying rhetorical anger another. Picasso need not have painted the whores at all, but it seemed a natural subject for someone who shared the late nineteenth century's sentimentalizing attitude toward such women, a kind of Baudelairean legacy. There can be little question that the sentimentalization of suffering gave a kind of market to such works—think of how moved audiences still are by cold, hunger, poverty, sickness, and death in *La Bohème*. John Richardson writes, "there is a hint of eroticism, even of sadism, to their portrayal." In a way, Picasso beautified the women because he relished the idea of a beautiful woman being caused to suffer. An ugly woman, or a woman rendered ugly by the harshness of her circumstances, blocks off the possibility of this perverted pleasure. Think, after all, of the history of depicting female victims, naked and chained to rocks, awaiting their rescuers. No one, presumably, would be erotically interested in rescuing a hag, or a woman shown starved and emaciated. But this means that by and large beauty in the depiction of such victims comes in for a moral criticism connected not so much with "the gaze" as with the fact that the gazer takes pleasure in the agonies of a beautiful female. So Picasso's works from this period are not altogether phony: they belong to a certain tradition, in which the use of beauty is perverse. Perhaps the right way to depict such victims, from a moral point of view, is to exclude any such pleasure and hence to exclude beauty in favor of documentation or indignation. In any case, it is important to recognize that, if this is true, it is incorrect, on Dorment's part, to speak of Picasso learning "to do without the consolation of visual beauty." Beauty in such cases is not a consolation but a relish, a device for enhancing the appetite, for taking pleasure in the spectacle of suffering. Indeed, Richardson says, "Picasso would describe women with some relish as 'suffering machines'." But that then raises the question of whether Picasso's subjects were not always victims of his style, of his imposing his will by rearranging their bodies to suit his appetite.

Against these considerations it is somewhat difficult to accept Dorment's assessment that Picasso's general eschewal of beauty "is what makes him an infinitely greater artist than Matisse," as if Matisse could not live without the "consolation." In truth, as I have argued, it would be very difficult to accept the claim that Matisse's *Blue Nude* is at all beautiful: she is fierce and powerful and sufficiently ugly that voyeurism seems ruled out, let alone arousal—almost as if the ugliness were a sort of veil of modesty with which Matisse covered her nakedness. Still, it is something of a critical commonplace that the work of Matisse's Nice period is inferior to his work from the period of *Blue Nude,* on just the grounds that it is almost floridly beautiful. I am not of that view at all. The beauty of these works is internal to their meaning. The world Matisse's works depict is a world of beauty, and the works themselves belong to the world they show. Matisse is absolutely coherent in this way, a hedonist and voluptuary rather than a sadist: he has sought to create a world which excludes suffering and hence the pleasure that might be taken in it. His characteristic corpus has the aesthetic quality of a medieval garden—a garden of love—from whose precincts everything inconsistent with the atmosphere of beauty has been walled off. To be in the presence of a Matisse is to look into that garden and to be in the presence of—the embodiment of—the spirit of the garden: a fragment of the earthly paradise. But what precisely is wrong with creating a place of beauty in a bad world? Matisse knew what the world is like. He created a sanctuary of beauty in his hotel room in Nice, with flowers and draperies and lovely women (and his own paintings on the easel or on the wall!) in much the same spirit, I would say, as those rooms in Istanbul that John Berger describes. They put the harshness of the world at a distance, and in that regard belong to the same space as the *Elegies*. This is what Matisse meant for his work to do.

I am extremely hesitant, on the basis of these considerations—or these considerations alone—to see Matisse as inferior to Picasso, let alone "infinitely" inferior, but Dorment's claim that he is so seems clearly based on some disapproval of beauty as an aesthetic quality to be at all sought after or used. As I see it, in his view beauty is a consolation, and consolation means mitigating the bitter truth, which it is morally more admirable to admit and to face than to deny. And to the degree that this represents the current attitude, it is not difficult to see what has happened to beauty in contemporary art. It is not art's business to console. Dorment's attitude is clearly in the spirit of the Intractable Avant-Garde. The relationship between art and society is that of irreconcilable antagonism, in which artistic beauty is bedding down with the enemy. But that is tantamount to an acknowledgment that beauty has the effect I have ascribed to it of consolation and mitigation, as in the paintings from Matisse's Nice period, the *Spanish Elegies,* the *Vietnam Veterans' Memorial*—or the post-9/11 shrines. It serves to put suffering in a kind of philosophical perspective.

Does the World Deserve Beauty?

I think it was in just such terms that Adam Verver must have viewed his museum for American City, as an island of light in the bleak world of an industrial city. It was in its way like a church. The church is a place of light and music and praise. Traditionally people bathed on Saturday night to make themselves clean for the Sabbath; and they changed into special clothing on Sunday morning when they entered its space, in symbolic acknowledgement of the moral difference between inside and outside, which metaphorically enacts the difference between the vale of tears in which human life is spent and the glorious kingdom that awaits them. But the contrast implied a certain acceptance of the way things are outside the church. Verver shows no sense of responsibility for changing the world that had made him a rich man, and for making daily life better for those whose labor enabled him to buy Damascene tiles and Siennese altarpieces for their aesthetic edification, let alone marrying a great beauty for his own aesthetic welfare. Why not instead put his money into hospitals and schools? Why not make the world outside the museum beautiful enough that the need for the compensatory beauty inside it disappears? With religion, it was possible to argue that the reason women bring children forth in pain and men earn their bread in the sweat of their brow is the original disobedience that drove our first parents out of paradise and into the harsh world they deserved. Life is a punishment. Beauty is for the life to come if we do our duty here. Who dares question the way of the Lord? But Verver lived on the cusp of the twentieth century. Why do we need to endure the world as it is, or mitigate it by building islands of beauty for intervals of relief, when we can mitigate it directly?

An argument can certainly be made that it would be a breach of morality to be philosophical about the things that seem instead to call for action and change. To say, in connection with sexual aggression against women, that well, men will be men, as if that were an eternal truth, is clearly wrong. Or, to take another case, there is clearly something wrong in using Christ's saying that the poor we shall always have with us as an excuse for doing nothing about the homeless. If beauty is linked with being philosophical, there are clear arguments against the moral appropriateness of beauty. And if art is internally linked with beauty, there is a moral argument against art. The artists of the 1993 Whitney Biennial could be grateful to the Intractable Avant-Garde for breaking that link. Why should they make beauty for a bad world?

The American painter Phillip Guston made lyrical abstractions in the 1950s and early 1960s, and then asked himself what right he had to be making beauty when the world was a scene of horrors, after which he painted allegorical political cartoons, with detached limbs and hooded figures smoking cigars. The question for Guston was how one could go on painting beautiful pictures when the

FIGURE 17   Philip Guston, *The Studio*, 1969
Completion without collaboration

world was falling apart. The pursuit of aesthetic purity was not an
acceptable option. He needed to find an art that was consistent
with his moral disquiet. "The Vietnam War was what was happening in America, the brutality of the world." And here his language
really does take on a lyrical intonation:

What kind of man am I, sitting at home, reading magazines, going
into a frustrated fury about everything—and then going into my

studio to *adjust a red to a blue*. I thought there must be some way I could do something about it. I knew ahead of me a road way laying. A very crude inchoate road. I wanted to be complete again, as I was when I was a kid.

Guston began to see his earlier style of painting as somehow no longer morally acceptable, given the way the world had gone. If there is to be art, it should not be beautiful, since the world as it is does not deserve beauty. Artistic truth must accordingly be as harsh and raw as human life itself is, and art leached of beauty serves in its own way as a mirror of what human beings have done. Art, subtracted of the stigma of beauty, serves as what the world has coming to it. Beautifiers are, so to speak, collaborationists.

Optional Beauty

But is there not a question of the appropriateness of art itself? For even if the art is not beautiful, art itself is already internally enough connected to philosophy that simply making art at all rather than acting directly where it is possible to act directly raises questions of moral priority. That is rather a dangerous question for philosophy, and hence precisely for just such a piece of writing as this. The *Spanish Elegies* put political loss in a philosophical perspective—but if that is wrong, how right can philosophy itself be, which puts *everything* in philosophical perspective?

I think the answer to this lies in what made Hegel think of art and philosophy as deflected forms of the same thing. Both were moments of what he termed Absolute Spirit, by which he means that in both of them—and in religion as the third such moment—spirit becomes its own subject, putting itself in perspective. The term "spirit" is sadly unavailable to us, but what Hegel is talking about is accessible enough. He is talking about self-knowledge—of the self's knowledge of its own deep reality. He felt that art was inferior to philosophy only in that it was dependent upon having to put its content into some sensory medium or other. But that need not concern us here. The important consideration is that art is one of the ways in which we represent ourselves for ourselves, which is why, after all, Hamlet spoke of art as a mirror. Philosophy is a struggle to put into words what we as human beings are in the most general terms we can find. We are *res cogitans*. We are machines. We are *Dasein*. We are *will-to-power*. We are *Geist*. It is very difficult, as we know, to visualize what the authors of these ideas mean. There really is no way of finding a picture that entirely captures these ideas, and Descartes was quite explicit that any picture was a falsification of what we really are. But Hamlet found a way of putting into a dramatic representation what he knew his uncle was—a poisoner, a fratricide—and to do it in such a way that the uncle not only recognized himself but knew that Hamlet knew a truth that the uncle had believed was hidden.

That is what the artists in the 1993 Biennial were attempting to do. They were presenting their fellow-Americans as victims and as victimizers. There was very little beauty in the show, but how, critically, could there have been if beauty would be incompatible with such contents? How could they be content to "adjust a red to a blue" when society seemed to them a scene of injustice and oppression? The difficulty was not with the individual items so much as with the sense that the entire show was like a market-place for grievances. It was like a congress of street-corner moralizers, each attempting to make the viewers conscious of their moral short-falls. But this was the fault, really, of the curators. Their show was certainly different from the Biennials of distant memory, with still-lifes, landscapes, nudes, interiors, and portraits—contents in connection with which beauty could be internally related. These were the traditional contents that the early modernists, whom Roger Fry had gathered together in the years just before the Great War, had presented in ways that were *not* beautiful. But the contents the artists of 1993 were addressing were not the traditional contents at all. Theirs were contents it would have been wrong to beautify. Their aim was to change people's moral attitudes. And beauty would have gotten in the way. It would have been artistically wrong.

The great consequence of beauty having been removed from the concept of art was that whether to use beauty or not became an option for artists. But that made it clear, or ought to have made it clear, that when and how to use beauty were matters governed by certain rules and conventions. That made a prediction that beauty was going to be the defining problem of the 1990s fairly chancy. More than beauty would be at issue. The 1993 Biennial may have been the high-water mark I have claimed it was. Or the Whitney learned a lesson about curating. Artists have always created for patrons—for princes and cardinals in one period, for businessmen in another. Ours is increasingly the age of the curator. The curator herself has been transformed from someone whose role, by etymological implication, was that of taking care of art, to someone whose imagination had in its own right a claim to art—an entrepreneurial spirit, creative in the discourse of exhibitions, put together for the benefit of the larger cultural consciousness, mirrors for the modern self. Some historian will want some time to track the causal route whereby curators replaced the kings and cardinals who had once been their patrons, and came to define the way our society would see art as well as what art it should see. To predict the way art will be is for the immediate future to predict what the interests of curators will be.

But there is a philosophical point to raise, having to do with the definition of art. It has been clear from the onset of modernism that something can be art without being beautiful. So beauty is not and cannot be part of the essence of art. Content, on the other hand, is a necessary condition for art, or at least I have so argued since *The Transfiguration of the Commonplace*. We have seen in this chapter that it is right or wrong to present certain contents as beautiful. This is so much the case that a cultural decision, if one were made, to have art that was beautiful would *ipso facto* be a decision as to what content art would have. In the twentieth century, disgust seemed the feeling appropriate to certain contents that might traditionally have been shunned when beauty seemed almost the default condition for art. As a default condition, it inevitably restricted what the content of art should be. The beauty of art reconciled viewers to a world seen in terms appropriate to it being viewed as beautiful. But there is a very wide range of feelings that artists have been called upon to arouse. When the revolutionary leaders urged David to paint the death of Marat—with which the art historian T.J. Clark has proposed that modernism begins—the aim was to arouse anger and indignation, and to increase revolutionary fervor and hatred against the enemies of revolution. The painters of the Counter-Reformation depicted the saints as suffering, in order to evoke pity. Sometimes beauty is compatible with these, sometimes it is not. If the aim of a painting is to arouse desire, it is appropriate that it be beautiful. If it is to arouse loathing, it is perhaps more appropriate that it be disgusting.

We have no specific term for these qualities. In the early theory of signs, the distinction was drawn between syntax, semantics, and pragmatics, the latter having to do with the relationship between signs and their interpreters. The latter term, clearly borrowed from "pragmatism," carried too heavy a burden of associations to simply call these qualities "pragmatic," though used in contrast with "semantic," it helps to note that pictures have typically been thought of in semantic terms, with reference to what they are pictures of, where pragmatics would instead draw attention to what the picture is intended to get viewers to *feel* toward the latter. "Beautification" is clearly pragmatic: it is intended to cause viewers to be more attracted to something than they would be without benefit of beautifiers. And that of course explains why beautification is regarded as tantamount to falsification. Charles K. Morris, to whom the theory of signs is due, observed that "rhetoric may be regarded as an early and restricted form of pragmatics."

It would be possible to designate the range of qualities to which beauty belongs as rhetorical, in that they dispose the viewer to take certain attitudes toward a given content. But "rhetorical" also carries too many associations for my purposes. The logician Frege uses the term "color"—"Farbung"—to designate the way terms are inflected by poets—and this comes close to characterizing the way beauty, for example, is used to cause viewers to have a certain attitude to what is shown. Perhaps it would be suitable to introduce "inflectors" as a term for this purpose.

In any case, the question that I merely raise at this point is whether it belongs to the definition of art that something is an artwork if it is inflected to cause an attitude to its content. Beauty has by far been the most important of the inflectors, but disgust would be another, and outrageousness a third. The readymades are not simply industrially produced found objects, but objects so inflected as to cause an attitude of aesthetic indifference. I won't say that the number of inflectors is boundless. But it is too great by far to suppose that even beauty, for all its credentials, will be the defining inflector for the art of the immediate future.

Nevertheless, if beauty is viewed as an inflector in art, then Hegel's marvelous thought—"Artistic beauty is born of the spirit and born again."—makes perfect sense. It goes from the artist's mind to the viewer's mind through the senses. Natural beauty is not born of the spirit, but it need not follow that natural and artistic beauty differ phenomenologically. The phenomenology of beauty is less important in the present study, however, than the recognition that the point of creating artistic beauty is not to abandon the viewer to its contemplation, but to grasp it as internal to the thought of the work. As, in my example, the use of beauty in the *Spanish Elegies* is to cause the viewer to feel an appropriate emotion about a form of political life that was vanquished many years ago now, that many hoped would have been beautiful had it survived and prevailed.

Whether we must widen the definition of art to make inflection a necessary condition need not be argued here. But at least inflection helps explain why we have art in the first place. We do so because, as human beings, we are driven by our feelings. Morris's thought that pragmatics is what had once been the discipline of rhetoric validates this thought, because the rhetoricians studied how to manipulate the feelings of their auditors, especially in law courts, to render the decisions they favored—or at least to be favorably disposed toward their client. So artists traditionally portrayed their subjects in such a way as to engage suitable feelings toward them on the part of the viewers—that they were powerful, kind, just, wise, fearful, or whatever. Or that they were holy persons, or pure souls, or deserved our compassion. When Hegel proclaimed the end of art, he supposed that we might now be more driven by reason than by feelings—but that would have meant, really, the end of a certain sort of humanity. What a suitably inflected work of art does is seduce the feelings of viewers and auditors, or to show that the subject as possessed of attributes that would on their own seduce those feelings. After all, people really are majestic or charismatic. If artists paint them that way, they are being true to the appearances. If not, than what they do is of a piece with beautification, a kind of falsification.

But these considerations explain why beauty itself is not the defining inflector it once was. When portraiture was a central genre of art, the primary media were painting and sculpture, both of which lend themselves in a natural way to mimetic practice, and hence the re-presentation of individual persons. And beauty itself is an attribute of individual persons, and hence of portraits, considered transparently. Where the person is insufficiently beautiful for rhetorical purposes, beautification is the natural recourse. But this can be generalized. There is a natural appetite for beauty, which meant that the subjects of the artist were expanded to include landscapes and still lifes, where natural and artistic beauty again coincide. Indeed, wherever this was true, there was subject matter for the artist. With religious paintings, especially in the Christian narrative, there were problems connected with martyrdom and crucifixions, imposing on artists a choice of transparency, in which case there would be blood and torn flesh, or beautification, as happened in the Renaissance. Beautification was a natural move when painting became taken up with narrative in general, since the scenes that were depicted would not in historical fact have been beautiful. Still, one was showing human beings in relationship to one another and in natural settings, so there was room for beautification. It may have been this that attracted Ruskin to the Pre-Raphaelites, because he so believed in visual truth. Beautification carries, as was argued earlier, an insinuation of falsification. But Ruskin was also a Victorian, which meant that he would find depictions of sex disgusting. That is what explains his giving the order that Turner's erotic studies should be burned. Indeed, he argued that they were symptoms of insanity. Members of the United States Congress in connection with Mapplethorpe's art used that kind of language—it was "sick."

Most of the work in the 1993 Biennial was made up of installations, and these would not naturally be objects of beauty, especially given their rhetorical intentions, namely to outrage visitors to the museum not at the art but at what the art represented. There has been less and less painting in the recent Biennials, and less and less of what would even in modernist times have been regarded as sculpture. These traditional genres play a decreasingly central role in the contemporary system of the arts, if there *is* a system of the arts today at all, when, as I began this book by observing, anything can be a work of art. But as the system has changed in recent times, beauty itself has less and less enjoyed the primacy that was taken for granted in the tradition of aesthetics we inherited. When aesthetics was changed, in the 1960s, beauty was scarcely mentioned.

It was premature, to say the least, to have proclaimed beauty the central issue of the 1990s—to declare, as one writer did—that "Beauty is back." Beauty is too humanly significant an attribute to vanish from life—or so one hopes. It can only become what it was once in art, however, if there is a revolution not just in taste, but also in life itself. That will have to begin with politics. When women are equal, when the races live in harmony and peace, when injustice has fled the world, then the kind of art the Whitney Biennial presents to a resentful world—this writer included!—will stop being made. Or when artists stop caring about these things, and just go back to painting for its own sake. Or if the world goes through so terrible a time that all that artists can do is comfort through elegy. Whatever the case, aesthetic attributes do not stand alone. They are part of much, much larger frameworks, for just the reason that art itself is inseparable from the rest of life. When one puts beauty in art in the context of life, then to predict that the beauty will be the issue of the future is implicitly to say that the whole of life, in which beauty plays its roles, will be the issue of the future. It is too vast a claim by far to be a matter merely of what art will be in the future.

6

Three Ways to Think
about Art

I once agreed to participate in a symposium organized as part of
the inaugural celebrations for an art school's new president. I did
so because a real exchange of views seemed an auspicious depar-
ture for an occasion otherwise merely ceremonial, with edifying
orations, the glee club, and a prim reception afterward—and
because the president is someone I quite admire and like. So I was
somewhat daunted to learn, some weeks after accepting the invita-
tion, that the subject was to be edifying after all—"The
Transformative Power of Art"—a title that, like "The Joy of
Creativity" or "Art and Human Freedom"—emitted the stale,
sour whiff of a commencement address. My initial impulse, like
Herr Goebbels upon hearing the word "culture," was to reach for
my revolver. But this was followed, almost immediately, with the
recognition that we—we at least in the artworld if not in the public relations or development offices of institutions of art education—almost never any longer talk about art in such terms at all.
Really, it occurred to me, we almost always talk about works of art
as objects—objects of a certain complexity to be sure, but objects
nonetheless. All at once, it struck me that the idea of transformative power connects with an aspect of art largely lost sight of in the
way art has become the subject of a professionalized body of discourses.

The way we think of museums today is largely connected with
these discourses, particularly since the abuse of beauty, together
with the subsequent disconnection of aesthetics from the discussion of art, left the role of the museum somewhat up in the air.
It is now viewed as a place for acquiring knowledge, and the
knowledge, as I previously noted, is of two kinds. One kind is the

knowledge of art as such, which in effect treats works of art as objects with an internal organization not unlike that of complex molecules. The other is the knowledge of art as a cultural product, where we visit the museum in order to see how the art of different cultures relate to the lives of those whose form of life they defined. This in effect is to see art in the way it is shown in anthropological museums—in dioramas, say, in which figures are shown in their native costumes, in settings which includes the gear by means of which they lived and the horizons that bounded their beliefs. One could in principle, I suppose, see the great museums of the western world—the Louvre, the Metropolitan, the Prado, the Uffizi—as anthropological museums, in which the culture happens to be our own.

In general, I think, the chief operative theory of art as knowledge of the first kind is one or another version of formalism. Formalism is no longer quite the favored posture for addressing works of art in museum and academic precincts that it had been in the 1960s, when we were invited, by critics and docents, mainly to consider diagonals and rhythms and internal references, similarities, repetitions, and the like. It offered, in the period of its ascendancy, ways of looking at art as objects internally composed under principles of design. Indeed, it was precisely to their design—their *disegno* to revert to a term used by Vasari—that Roger Fry appealed as the basis for judging the excellence of Post-Impressionist paintings. As such, formalism yielded a universal mode of understanding any work whatever, irrespective of its historical or cultural origin, and it, more than anything, dissolved the progressive model of artistic development, which had lasted from the Renaissance through the end of the nineteenth century. It liberated museums from the format of organizing art into national schools, which so inspired Hegel, and within schools into succeeding historical periods. Under formalist analysis, objects could be compared with one another in point of visual organization, as in the standard two-projector lecture, where one is directed to note affinities and discontinuities, and to exercise ones discriminatory powers. Art-objects could be juxtaposed irrespective of provenance, and one could trace their points of resemblance in the air as one's audience scanned the paired images on the screen. One could group objects together to "communicate with one another" in exhibitions which might contain Persian pots, Baule masks,

Renaissance bronzes, a piece of fiber art by Ann Hamilton, and some Navajo weavings—works which have no connection with one another except as art objects perceived to have this or that affinity. I would go out of my way to see a show with some such contemporary title as *Beauty Matters*, composed of just such a heterogeneous array of artworks. It could be a demonstration, perhaps, that beauty is much the same everywhere, irrespective of culture and history—though whether the beauty were internal or external could hardly be raised, let alone resolved, on formalist principles alone.

"Formalism permitted me," one of our rightly most celebrated critics and scholars of modern art once declared, "to separate myself from the type of subjective, romantic and poetic criticism practiced, among others, by Harold Rosenberg." That means, it seems to me, that the focus of her interest was on a kind of syntactic inquiry into works of art considered objectively—that is, as objects with certain resident structures it was the task of the critic to identify and clarify, independent of any external reference—of semantics, so to speak—and in particular of any pragmatic reference to those who experience them. She was speaking of criticism as a kind of autonomous *Kunstswissenschafft*—almost in the spirit of positivism—practiced by experts. Artistic Formalism, so considered could have been the subject of a monograph in that canonical work of Logical Positivism, *The Encyclopedia of Unified Science*—in which Charles Morris's influential *Foundations of A Theory of Signs,* cited at the end of the previous chapter, was first published.

I think it is very valuable for students to learn how to look at works of art as formal exercises, to "look under the hood" as the scholar I have just quoted—it is of course Rosalind Krauss—puts it in a study of the work of Cindy Sherman. That was not my way of thinking of Sherman's work—I happen to have a taste for "subjective, romantic, and poetic" responses—and feel I learn a lot about art from reading that kind of criticism, as well, of course, as the writings of Krauss herself, or her disavowed mentor, Clement Greenberg, on individual works of art. Consider, for example, the profound response to an archaic torso of Apollo by the poet Rilke. Rilke describes a downward curve in the figure's torso, but hardly in the spirit of a formalist observation. The curve leads down to the limbless figure's genital area, and it really does not matter that the genitals themselves might have been broken off long ago, in the spirit of iconoclasm or perhaps to secure a sexual talisman. Actual stone genitals are no more important to Rilke's experience than the statue's head, which is also missing. We do not see the figure's eyes, but somehow we feel ourselves seen by the entire body—"there is no spot that does not look at you." And for the same reason, there is no spot that is *not* genital: the whole torso expresses a sexual energy so powerful that that the poet sees himself as a very weak, very wanting sort of being. In the ferocity of the god's thrusting strength, the poet cannot help but ask what kind of a man he himself is. If it were a woman, I should think, there would be a sense that her lover must be replaced, or that something in her has been awakened that only a god could satisfy. "You have to change your life," with which the poem ends, is the crushing thought induced by seeing oneself in the perspective of the god's body.

Disturbing as it is, it is an experience one would want to have if one could. Put in general terms, it is what, having read Rilke's poem, would send one to the gallery of antiquities, not to learn about the evolution of "the Apollo figure" but to be addressed and challenged from across the millennia. Yet there are limits to what we can turn ourselves into. What after all did Rilke himself do? He wrote the poem. It is a poem at the very least about how a work of art can get us to ask what we are, and what we must in the end settle for, given our human dimensions. "You are what you understand," the tremendous *Erdgeist* tells Faust, who cringed before her. This may itself be a "subjective, romantic, poetic" response to Rilke's poem. One can look under the poem's hood, and acknowledge its sonnet-like structure. But if the poem does not have something like the effect on the reader that the sculpture had on the poet, something has failed.

Let us turn to the other kind of knowledge, which has become increasingly important to the art profession since, and partly as the cause of the weakening of the formalist model. We see art as referring to and expressing the inner life of a culture. Tramping through the Rijksmuseum in Amsterdam once, I made my way among clumps of cognitive pilgrims, addressed in various languages, and it became clear to me that the purpose of their being there had less to do with disinterested contemplation than with acquiring information and experience, much like our eighteenth-century predecessors on the grand tour. What was the knowledge for? Well, these twentieth-century tourists learned a lot about seventeenth-century Dutch culture. And listening to their docents, I learned a lot as well. One docent unpacked a marriage portrait, from which I learned something about how married love was portrayed in those days. But in the end I felt that the Dutch were being treated as a tribe like the Trobriand Islanders. And I then thought about the American tribe, to which I belong. But no painting tells more about what it is to live American culture than the movies, the sit-com, the popular music, the dances, the clothing, the hair-styles, the automobiles, the plumbing, the guides to sex and stock investment—all those semiotic systems which define our form of life. In a newspaper interview in 1915, Duchamp said

> The capitals of the Old World have labored for hundreds of years to find that which constitutes good taste and one may say that they have found the zenith thereof. But why do people not understand what a bore this is? . . . If only America would realize that the art of Europe is finished—dead—and that America is the country of the art of the future . . . Look at the skyscrapers! Has Europe anything to show more beautiful than these? New York itself is a work of art, a complete work of art . . .

And of course he famously said that America's great contribution to civilization was modern plumbing.

There was an exhibition recently titled *Kitchen and Bathroom/The Aesthetics of Waste*. It showed the evolution of these two rooms so central to modern domesticity, once appliances became available in the nick of time to replace servants. Advertisement after advertisement from the 1930s and 1940s showed perky wives in pretty aprons, loading washing machines, brewing coffee, using the toastmaster, serving their husbands. The bathroom was filled with hard shiny surfaces, easy to clean. If one opened the cupboards or refrigerator, one would behold prepared foods, which took the drudgery out of cooking—all one needed to do was add water and heat. Feminism casts a backward illumination under which women were domestic slaves, which perhaps connects the kitchen with the paintings of Hopper, showing a lonelier America. But they show it in no way better than the advertisements in womens' magazines themselves show it—or than bathroom fixtures and kitchen appliances do.

For the matter, then, one could make American culture available without putting into a show any works of art at all—as with the famous 1969 exhibition, *Harlem on my Mind,* at the Metropolitan Museum of Art, in which all that was on view were enlarged photographs of Harlem, with Cotton Club music piped into the galleries. That show was exceedingly controversial. Harlem artists were outraged. The Jewish Defense League was outraged by the anti-Semitic implications of the catalogue. The critics were outraged that a great art museum had been turned into an annex of the museum of natural history. But that is what the second model does. It anthropologizes art. However, art is no better for these purposes than cook books, Polaroids, the Sears Roebuck catalog. So what is the point of an *art* museum, filled with expensive fragile objects collected by various rich persons for their private taste, and turned over to the public in exchange for tax benefits?

Art's Transformative Power

There is a characteristically hectoring and in the context unsettling image by Barbara Kruger, installed in the lower lobby of the Wexner Center for the Arts in Ohio State University. A woman is shown holding her hands to her head, like the screaming figure in Munch's celebrated painting. White letters on a red banner ask: Why are you here? Kruger's questions always throw us off balance, especially when she follows them up.

Here she asks: To kill time? To get cultured? To widen your world? To improve your social life? These are not contemptible motives. When I first moved to New York, one could almost always count on meeting someone nice in front of Picasso's *Guernica*, at the time in the Museum of Modern Art. That was before the bar scenes, or the personals ads in the New York Review of Books. Did the art do more than confer on the site a certain elevating tone, guaranteeing that those we meet are likely to be our sorts of person? Or give us something we can break the ice with by talking about it in its presence? A story by Don de Lillo about a pick up, admittedly a not very satisfying one, involves a man and a woman who talk to one another—who cannot help talking to one another—in a gallery in which Gerhard Richter's *17 October, 1978* is displayed, which depicts the prison deaths of members of the

FIGURE 18   Barbara Kruger, *Untitled (Why Are You Here?)*, 1991
To be transformed?

Baader-Meinhof Gang. If it means the same thing to you as it does to me, the characters seem to think, then perhaps, just perhaps, there is hope of some deeper bond.

It would be wonderful if we could in honesty respond to Kruger's questions by saying: We are here to be transformed. We have come here to become different persons. And this brings me back to the topic of The Transformative Power of Art. Having said all this, it is undeniable that transformation or something like transformation is occasionally an effect that art has on those who encounter it, and I was too good a guest, finally, not to register this truth, and to try to connect it with the teaching of art. I had been thinking, as it happened, about Maya Lin's *Vietnam Veterans' Memorial,* Though the work has a complexity connected with its site, its occasion, and with tragedy and memory—there is no question in my mind that its beauty, as I proposed in Chapter 4, is internally related to the profound effect it has on those who come to mourn, but also on those who merely come to experience it as a profound work of art. Maya Lin has recently described how the idea of the memorial formed in her mind, and I thought it particularly suitable to observe that it came out of an undergraduate seminar in funerary architecture at Yale, and a class expedition to the Mall in Washington, D.C. That connected it with the art school as an institution, and it gave the concept of transformation legitimacy as a theme for the occasion we were celebrating.

How many of the students were likely to become transformative is difficult to say. Mostly the school will turn out the art-workers the society needs—designers and teachers, photographers and filmmakers, craftspersons and draughtspersons. But how many of my own students in philosophy are destined to be Platos or Kants or Wittgensteins? When one talks about philosophy in an educational context, one does so in terms of what Hegel calls, in talking about art, its "highest vocation." Still, the *Vietnam Veterans' Memorial* stands as a challenge to the entire complex of attitudes toward artworks as objects, with which I began. More than this, I think, the *Memorial* emblematizes the role that art plays in most of our lives, even if we happen to be members of the cognitive art establishment. In his remarkable book, *Painting as an Art,* Richard Wollheim has this to say: "Many art historians make do with a psychology that, if they tried to live their lives by it, would leave them at the end of an ordinary day without lovers, friends, or any insight into how this had come about." We need only think of quite ordinary works and what they mean to us to realize how inadequate most of what is written and taught about art is for explaining how this happens. My own life has been transformed by reading Proust or Henry James, both of whose works have made me a quite different person from what I would have been had I not read at all, or had never encountered them. Proust's novel teems with characters who see their lives in terms of paintings, stories, melodies, bits of architecture, gardens, essays. I have the view that they are transfigured by seeing themselves in the framework of these works.   But everyone can talk about how his or her life was changed by a movie or a play or even simple piece of visual art. I remember how the very modern heroine of one of Margaret Atwood's novels was moved to tears by a simple print of happy peasants harvesting vegetables in China at the time of Mao.

Do these considerations help in any way in meeting Kruger's confrontational question? Or is her question addressed more to the museum as a cognitive establishment, not all that different, when one thinks about it, from the university itself, especially in connection with its humanistic wing, which does not have especially good answers to the question of why students should pay high tuitions to study works of art as objects? What, really, without taking refuge in the edifying discourse to which the very issue of "The Transformative Power of Art " belongs, are presidents of institutions of higher learning to say? Kruger, we appreciate, is by her own example concerned that there be an art that, to use an expression of Claes Oldenberg, does something more than sits on its ass in some museum or other. Her images enter the stream of life, they raise hell, which is part of what makes the image she did for the Wexner Center somehow disconcerting and ungrateful, and even subversive. She does not want us to study her works as objects. She wants us to change our lives for the better through their agency— to lead better lives, to treat one another with greater dignity. But what then is the museum to do? *Her* objects enter life through the gift shop, as coffee mugs and tote bags, bearing their political messages into the streets and on to kitchen counters. But is this really what we want from art, or for the matter from the museum?

What Do Art Museums Want?

In a widely discussed article in the *New York Times,* the critic Roberta Smith raised a question not unlike Kruger's, but addressed not to museum visitors, but to museums themselves: Why are you here? Smith asks "What do art museums want?" It cannot be a coincidence that her question paraphrases Freud's infamous "What do women want?" Her question, she feels, has a particular urgency at a moment when museums seem to "want to be anything but art museums?" What I believe bothers her—and the tenor of her text expresses this—is that art museums want as

institutions to be what Barbara Kruger wants art to be. They want
the way they show art to change the lives of those who use them.
This, I think, is what Smith means by saying that they want to be
"anything but art museums." My sense is that Smith's concern
reflects the transition from the first model of the museum as an
institution of knowledge to the second model—from seeing the
museum as a place where we learn to understand art to one where
we use art to learn about the cultures art is part of—from art as an
end to art as a means. I belong to a generation that went to the
museum as a kind of sanctuary, where one simply took great satisfaction in looking at what one saw there, without reference to
learning anything much at all. The museum where I grew up was
a quiet empty place with fascinating pictures in gold frames. I
never much looked under the hood, and I knew too little of history to connect what I saw with distant events. In a way, looking
at art was like reading books. I never asked why the museum was
there, or who paid for it. If someone were to have asked me, in the
spirit of Barbara Kruger, Why are you here?, I am not sure I could
have given much of an answer. It would be like having to answer
why I walked along the beach. It was just one of life's pleasures.
But you could not get very far with city councils, let alone national
endowments, without some better justification than that.

Smith picked out for particular notice an instructively controversial exhibition, *Made in California: Art, Image, and Identity,
1900–2000,* installed at the Los Angeles County Museum to mark
the end of the century. It sought "to place art and artists within a
particular historical, political, social, and economic context,"
according to the Foreword to the exhibition's catalog, written by
the LACMA's director, Andrea Rich. What the exhibition in effect
did was to strip works of art from their privileged position in society by treating them as simply part of visual culture, expressing the
society they were part of, but no differently than an other part of
California's visual culture—the clothes, the houses, the cars, the
roads—California the way the museum of Natural History treats
Borneo or New Guinea, using the art as cultural indices. Visitors
from New Guinea or Borneo—or from distant planets—could use
the exhibition as a way of finding out about how the Californians
lived in their exotic culture. Critics could and obviously did say, in
effect, that artworks are not just artifacts, and that to treat them as
such is to put those who view them in just the wrong relationship

to what they see. I shall return to this in a moment, but I want also to point to the Kruger-like questions the curators put: "Which California?" "Whose California?" Like Kruger's, these questions are intended to put us, at least if we are Californians, off balance. The exhibition set out to show that the California presented in the art was not necessarily the California that everyone living in California actually lived. It implicitly criticized the art because of that. The show gave Californians a mirror in which to see themselves. It was a cracked mirror—or a cracked society. The museum in a way turned itself into an agency for transforming its viewers into critics of the society that supported the museum. Trustees may ask: Is this what our taxes are paying for? Is this what art should be used for? At the very least the curators were asking if the taxes should all go to support an art that represented but part of the population of the state. Ought not all parts of it be represented? Not just the art of the white middle class, but of Chicanos and Blacks and the Chinese and Japanese that are also California?

Made in California had a point, but it depressed me to think about it. It did so because it put a lot of the art I loved in a perspective that had nothing to do with why I loved it. It made it into social-science specimens, products of a certain class and race. That was not the way I had thought and written about Richard Diebenkorn's paintings, or those of Joan Brown or Elmer Bischof or Richard Arneson or Robert Irwin or Ed Kienholz. As a New Yorker, I take a definite pride in the art of the New York School. But I don't think of it as "our" art. I think it belongs to the world. Probably, *Made in California* was a tacit plea for artistic multiculturalism, a way of saying that there are a lot of Californias, not just the California of the Bay area and Los Angeles art-worlds.

I once aired these issues in a talk for an organization of museum directors by using some ideas of the Hegel that I have always found valuable. Hegel's central concept is that of *Geist,* which literally translates as "spirit," though the latter term is too associated with communications from a world beyond to capture what he meant. Let's just translate *Geist* as "mind." Hegel distinguished "subjective mind"—the mind that connects with the body in some deeply un-understood and possibly, as the philosopher Colin McGinn has argued, un-understandable way—from what he called *objective* mind. This consists in all the objects, practices, and institutions which together define a form of life actually lived. These are products of mind and not of nature, and are internalized by those educated in the conduct of life. A form of life that is complex enough that human beings can live it will always have something in it we can think of as art, whatever meaning may be assigned it by those in whose life it figures. Objective spirit lends itself as a concept to the "art as cultural index model," as it does to multiculturalism. It is an idea taken up as iconology by Professor Panofsky, who uses the example, as I recall it, of tipping a hat as a way into our system of meanings, which exposes him to the question of what the purpose of art can be for the iconologist other than as further elements in the language of the culture. Even perspective, for Panofsky, was a symbolic form. It represents a certain cultural decision, to represent the objective world spatially in terms the orderly recession of objects in space. That does not make perspective a convention. For we in fact do perceive the world perspectively—we really do see railway tracks converging at the horizon. That is the way our optical system is made. Perspective was *discovered* in the sense that Brunelleschi *learned* how to show things the way they are actually seen. Still, it was a cultural decision to show them that way. When perspective was explained to the Chinese, they saw right away that that is the way we see. But they had no interest in using it for their own artistic ends. It had nothing to do with the way art fit into their culture. Their eyes were like our eyes. But the "objective spirit" of China was different from that of *quattrocento* Florence.

Hegel had another concept of mind—what he termed *Absolute Spirit*. There were, he thought, three "moments" of Absolute Spirit: art, religion, and philosophy. Art made palpable the highest values of the human spirit, and in a sense showed human beings what it meant for them to be bearers of these values. It translated religious beliefs into sensuous images. The temple and the cathedral thus expressed their cultures, but they did something more than this: they expressed the vision of the world under which the people of those cultures lived. But in this way, art performed a philosophical function. It *was* philosophy in a displaced form. Hegel famously felt that this was no longer a possibility for art, that it had been superseded by philosophy for persons who no longer needed illustrative images to understand its propositions. This was his notorious "End of Art" thesis, which I have frequently alluded to in these pages, and a variant of which I have discussed in my own writings.

Now my own version of the end of art is not like Hegel's in the sense that I do not think that art has been superseded by philosophy. Philosophy is simply hopeless in dealing with the large human issues. When I think of those Dutch marriage portraits—or of Van Eyck's portrait of the Arnolfini couple—against what philosophers have said on the topic of marriage, I am almost ashamed of my discipline. Kant, who knew nothing of marriage as a lived state, defined it in *The Metaphysics of Morals* as "the union of two persons of different sexes for the purpose of lifelong mutual possession *of one another's sexual organs,*" which is more a coarse joke for a peasant wedding than a considered proposition in the metaphysics of matrimony. Kant does add, to this reductive characterization, that procreation cannot be the entire story "for otherwise the marriage would dissolve of its own accord when procreation ceases"—but he never offers a positive account to guide persons in an age like our own when procreation and what he characterizes (in Latin, of course) as *usus membrorum et facultatum sexualium alterius* are, while not exactly neither here nor there, not entirely at the heart of the matter either, since both are available to couples who still ponder the option of marriage. A dear friend who once contemplated suicide asked whether I could direct him to some philosophical text that could help him decide whether to go on living, and I could not. What philosophy does is try to put the whole of everything in some kind of metaphysical nutshell. But it really aspires to universality.

I told the museum directors about an exhibition I had discussed with a young curator, which seemed to me to exemplify what it might mean to think of art as doing what philosophy tries, or ought to try to do, but in a concrete way, with what Hegel would dismiss as sensuous objects. The curator originally titled his show *The Vanitas Theme in Contemporary Art,* but had begun to think of calling it *Meditations on Beauty and Death.* There is, as I have sought to show, a connection between beauty and death in that it is through beauty that we vest death with meaning, as in funeral ceremonies, with flowers and music and fine ceremonial words. Kant writes that death is appropriately expressed by means of a "beautiful genius." Perhaps beauty confers meaning on life in much the same way, as though its existence validates life. I once wrote about a Tibetan *tanka* which shows the death of Buddha. The Buddha dies in a garden, in a beautiful pavilion, surrounded by plantings, on a beautiful day. He says farewell to the world at its most beautiful, which is when a Buddha would choose to die: the beauty of the world that holds lesser persons back from fulfilling their higher purposes. That is what the *vanitas* form is all about. It often is a still life in which a skull is surrounded by beautiful objects which the painting means to tell us are vain, are distractions, are ephemeral. The term *vanitas* means "nothing." And of course under Christianity one is urged not to be distracted, whatever the temptations, and to fix ones mind on the next world. Thus the connection between beauty and death. That connection is extended by this exhibition into works very different from the Dutch *vanitas* of the seventeenth century. There is, for example, a work by Felix Gonzales-Torres, consisting of two identical clocks, which keep time synchronously. They are very modern clocks, of the kind that would hang in a kitchen or a schoolroom, though hardly as a pair. Who needs two clocks? One could always check one against the other, but which one would one trust? The fact that there is a pair of them means that Gonzales-Torres is not pre-senting them as a "readymade." In fact Torres was saying some-thing about love and marriage. One of the clocks will stop running before the other. Time will stop for it before it stops for its mate.

FIGURE 19 Felix Gonzales-Torres, *Untitled (Perfect Lovers)*, 1991
One will die before the other.

It would be a beautiful thing if they both stopped running on the same tick, as it were, like a couple dying in unison. Gonzales-Torres's lover had died of AIDS, as he himself was to do not much later. It is a memorial and a monument at once to the idea of "till death do us part" which is built into our concept of the meaning of marriage. It is a very tender, and very moving piece of art. It is a meditation. But as a "meditation," a genre of philosophizing, it connects with the great mysteries of human life and meaning. It is interesting to see the two clocks as a *vanitas*. It helps us understand why we need contemporary art to address these questions for contemporary men and women. The forms are different from culture to culture, but the questions transcend difference in culture. No culture is without a way of dealing with death, or a strategy for handling suffering. And that I feel is what the concept of Absolute Spirit is about. It connects the art of a given culture with humanity in the largest sense of the term.

Artworks As Embodied Meanings

I have a different model than either of the two with which I began this chapter. It is the model of *embodied meanings*. It is a model I use as an art critic all the time, trying to say what a given work means, and how that meaning is embodied in the material object which carries it. What I have in mind is what the thought is that the work expresses in non-verbal ways. We must endeavor to grasp the thought of the work, based on the way the work is organized. Let me give an example of how I like to proceed.

The Museum of the Rhode Island School of Design in Providence decided to celebrate its 125th birthday by inviting a number of individuals to write a short statement about one of the works in its collection that they particularly admire. The idea was to put the statements up next to the work described, so that visitors can read how someone thinks about the piece that they are looking at. I selected a painting by one of my favorite artists, the Dutch Mannerist, Joachim Wtewael. There is something crazy about Wtewael's work, and beyond question it represents an eccentric taste on my part that I go out of my way to see his paintings whenever I can. The RISD Museum has a great Wtewael, which represents the wedding of Peleus and Thetis, for most Americans a fairly obscure motif.

FIGURE 20   Joachim Wtewael, *The Wedding of Peleus and Thetis*, 1610
A mortal among immortals

The painting is not in great condition, being somewhat the worse for having been restored. One can see that it is beautifully painted, but I defer for the moment any aesthetic opinion, other than to say that it is exuberantly—or perhaps exquisitely—mannerist.

Whenever I spend time with one of Wtewael's oblique and arcane works, I try to feel myself addressed as part of the rare and refined audience for whom he must have painted. It was an audience that expected the meaning of art to be concealed but accessible, so Wtewael's pictures are elegant mazes, tissues of delicate references and implications that challenged the learning and flattered the sophistication of his patrons. He expected them to know the stories—to know, in the *The Wedding of Peleus and Thetis*, what brought bride and groom together and who the guests were, and why the subject was worth painting. I like to imagine a group of worldly Dutch men and women, members, historically speaking, of the Dutch aristocracy, seated at a table, dressed in garments as stylish as the painting itself, challenging one another's interpretations the way we do when we talk about an artful film or novel. Their table is a still life of crusts and fruit peels, and partly empty goblets. Wtewael's painting hangs in the room, and it is luminous under candle flame and firelight reflected from mirrors and polished cupboards, pearls and satin skirts, and it hangs in their midst like a vision of peace and pleasure. As in the painting, there is a sleeping dog, indifferent to the witty toasts, the manneristic compliments to host and hostess, and to the merriment the topic of marriage always arouses. The men and women know that the wily Thetis metamorphosed herself through a sequence of scary forms before yielding to Peleus, and that the chief gods allowed Peleus— a mortal—to marry the beautiful sea nymph only because her son was fated to be stronger than his father. Their son in fact was to be the great hero Achilles, mostly a god, marginally but decisively mortal. But why is Peleus shown so much older than his delicious bride? Plenty of room there for ribald speculation and whispered innuendos! And there is another joke: it would be a pretty puny son that would find difficulty in besting this senior citizen with the receded hairline. Actually, Peleus looks something like me, and someone might tease me by saying that what I like about the painting is the fact that it shows a man of my age and looks, with his arm around the waist of a very pretty young woman, both of us as naked as pagans.

The bridal pair is seated in the place of honor at a festive table with fruits and goblets and flowers, and all the other guests are gods and goddesses. That gives a deep reason why Peleus looks as old as he does. He is the only one in the picture who will age, and the only one who will die. The rest are immortal. So the picture in a strange way is something of a *vanitas*. The poet Sappho said that we know from the gods that death is a bad thing—for if it were a good thing, the gods themselves would die. The gods have youthful beautiful bodies and live without fear of what we fear every day of our brief lives.

The Dutch, knowing their Ovid, are aware that terrible times lie ahead. All the gods save one have been invited to the celebration. The uninvited guest—Eris, goddess of disorder—is about to throw a golden apple onto the table. On it was written "To the most beautiful"—but which of the goddesses was that? Juno, the goddess of power, Minerva the goddess of wisdom, or Venus the goddess of erotic love? Everyone knew what happened after that— a world torn apart, the golden age, in which gods and mortals married one another and sat down to share a meal, was irremediably shattered. It was in fact the last occasion on which gods and mortals sat down with one another to table. If only someone could stop Eris! It is a characteristic of Mannerist compositions that the central figure is difficult to identify. In Bruegel's *Landscape with the Fall of Icarus*, Icarus is a tiny pair of legs that could belong to a diver, an incidental detail. The Ploughman is the foreground figure, but the painting is not about him except in the sense that he is going on about his business, entirely unaware of the tremendous failure of a boy falling out of the sky. He tried to emulate a god— Apollo—and drowned in the attempt. Which one is Eris? Where is the apple of discord? And what does the story of this last supper mean for us, sitting here in our castle, on top of the world, enjoying the good things of life—art, wine, tasty things to eat, and one another's company?

Is the painting beautiful? Well, of course it is beautiful in the way Mannerism defined beauty—elegant and ornamental, like the gods and goddesses Wtewael shows. Its beauty is internal; in the way I earlier argued Matisse's paintings from his Nice period are beautiful. They themselves belong in the reality Matisse painted. If the svelte and slender immortals had paintings, they would look the way Wtewael's paintings look. Is it a transformative work of art? I don't truly know. But I know that if it is to transform its viewers, they need to see it as something more than an example of what the Dutch aristocratic class around Utrecht in the late sixteenth century wanted to be surrounded with. And I cannot imagine what it would be to look under the hood of the painting without knowing its meaning. The meaning, if I have it right, is philosophical, and internally related to its viewers. It put their lives in perspective. It tells them what, really, they already know.

7

Beauty and Sublimity

In 1948, *The Tiger's Eye*—an influential magazine devoted to literature and the arts—published a symposium titled "Six Opinions on What is Sublime in Art?" There had been little of note written on this topic since Hegel's lectures on aesthetics in the 1820s, but it must have seemed to the editors of the magazine, who were very close to the Abstract Expressionist movement, that something was beginning to happen in painting that put it in candidacy for sublimity. Two of the movement's more intellectual figures—Robert Motherwell and Barnett Newman—were among the symposiasts, but it was Newman who wrote with an excitement and conviction that the title of his contribution perfectly conveys: "The Sublime is Now." Early that year, allegedly on his forty-third birthday—January 29th, 1948—Newman had made what he regarded as a major breakthrough, not only in his own painting, but in painting as such, with a work he was to call *Onement I.* There can be little question, I think, that Newman connected this work with the tremendousness conveyed by the idea of the sublime. It was somehow too momentous an achievement, in his mind at least, to think of as merely beautiful, or beautiful, really, at all. Some decades later, the post-modernist thinker, Jean-François Lyotard, was to write that in the "aesthetic of the sublime . . . the logic of the avant-garde finds its axioms." And it is clear from the way in which Newman polarizes the two concepts, that he saw no possibility of finding the axioms of his art in the aesthetic of the beautiful. If there was to be an aesthetic for *Onement I,* nothing less than the sublime would suffice. There are, as I have pointed out, a great many aesthetic qualities other than beauty. But none of them poses

FIGURE 21
Barnett Newman,
Onement I, 1948
**Beyond mere
beauty**

quite the challenge to beauty that sublimity does, and I shall close my discussion of the abuse of beauty with this last chapter in its history.

Avant-garde intellectuals, in mid-twentieth-century America, and especially in New York, inevitably saw the world in terms of polar opposition. This was doubtless a consequence of having been brought up on the *Communist Manifesto,* in which society is dramatically portrayed as now split into "two great hostile classes facing each other: Bourgeoisie and Proletariat." The subtext of

Greenberg's "Avant-Garde and Kitsch," for example, was the struggle between two incompatible philosophies of culture which he respectively identified with Fascism (= Kitsch) and Socialism (= Avant-Garde). Philip Rahv, an editor of the influential *Partisan Review*, in which Greenberg's essay had been published, spoke of American writers as grouped into two polar types: "Paleface and Redskin," exemplified respectively by Henry James and Walt Whitman. Newman could not resist placing the sublime with the beautiful in polar contrast with one another:

> The invention of beauty by the Greeks, that is, their postulate of beauty as an ideal, has been the bugbear of European art and European aesthetic philosophies. Man's natural desire in the arts to express his relation to the Absolute became confused and identified with the absolutisms of perfect creations—with the fetish of quality—so that the European artist has been continually involved in the moral struggle between notions of beauty and the desire for sublimity.

With equal inevitability, Newman sees the history of art as an aesthetic struggle, between "the exaltation to be found in perfect form" on the one side, and, on the other, "the desire to destroy form, where form can be formless." It is, he argues, "The impulse of modern art to destroy beauty," which has precisely been the argument of this book.

American Sublime

Newman framed the polarity between beauty and sublimity within another polarity, that between Europe and America. "The failure of European art to achieve the sublime is due to this blind desire . . . to build an art within a framework of the Greek ideal of beauty." This is because European art was "unable to move away from the Renaissance imagery of figures and objects except by distortion or by denying it completely for an empty world of geometrical formalisms." But—"I believe that here in America, some of us, free from the weight of European culture, are finding the answer, by completely denying that art has any concern with the problem of beauty and where to find it." This opposition between Europe and America is echoed by Robert Motherwell, the only American in the movement in fact to have visited Europe, and whose sensibility among masters of the New York School owed most to a kind of European culture. It was Motherwell who invented the term "The New York School" to distinguish what he and his peers were doing from "The School of Paris." And in an important interview of 1968, Motherwell said: "I think that one of the major American contributions to modern art is sheer size. There are lots of arguments as to whether it should be credited to Pollock, Still, Rothko, even Newman . . . The surrealist tone and literary qualities were dropped, and [it was] transformed into something plastic, mysterious, and sublime. No Parisian is a sublime painter, nor a monumental one."

Let me round off my little catalog of polarities by reverting to Rahv. "While the redskin glories in his Americanism, to the paleface it is a source of endless ambiguities." James may have been a paleface, but he tirelessly pursued the moral allegory of the culturally and morally innocent American among the sophisticated (and corrupt) Europeans. He could not resist giving the hero of his 1877 novel, *The American,* the allegorical name "Newman." The New Man has come to the Old World on a cultural pilgrimage in 1868, having made his fortune manufacturing wash tubs; and James has a bit of fun at his hero's expense by inflicting him with an "aesthetic headache" in the Louvre, where his story begins. "I know very little about pictures or how they are painted," Newman concedes; and as evidence, James has him ordering, as if buying shirts, half a dozen copies of assorted old masters from a pretty young copyist who thinks he is crazy, since, as she puts it, "I paint like a cat."

By a delicious historical coincidence, Barnett Newman—another New Man—visits the Louvre for the first time in 1968, exactly a century later. By contrast with James's hero, this Newman has had the benefit of having read Clement Greenberg and had himself gone through a Surrealist phase. So he is able to tell his somewhat patronizing guide—the French critic Pierre Schneider—to see Uccello's *The Battle of San Romano* as "a modern painting, a flat painting," and to explain why Mantegna's Saint Sebastian bleeds no more than a piece of wood despite being pierced with arrows. He sees Géricault's *Raft of the Medusa* as 'tipped up' like one of Cézanne's tables—"It has the kind of modern space you wouldn't expect with that kind of rhetoric." And in general the new New Man is able to show European aesthetes a thing or two about how to talk about the Old Masters—and incidentally how to look at his own work, which so many even of his New York School contemporaries found intractable. In Rembrandt, for example, Newman sees "All that brown, with a streak of light coming down the middle of them—as in my own painting." His guide, the critic Pierre Schneider, European to the core, pretends to see Newman as a redskin—"a noble savage with a protective disguise, just as the Huron, to be left in peace, pretends to be an oilman."

Surpassing Every Standard of Sense

Beauty had been put on the defensive as early as the eighteenth century, when the concept of the sublime first entered Enlightenment consciousness through the translation by Boileau of a text on the subject by a somewhat obscure rhetorician, traditionally known as Longinus; and *A Philosophical Enquiry into the Origin of the Sublime and the Beautiful,* by the Irish statesman, Edmund Burke. Beauty, in the Enlightenment had become inextricably connected with taste, and refined taste was the defining mark of aesthetic cultivation. Aesthetic education implies that there are rules that one can learn, as in moral education, though it would be expected that in both, the pupil will in time be on his or her own, and know when something is beautiful or right respectively through having acquired good taste in each. It was entirely correct of Newman to connect the idea of beauty with perfection. The mark of the sublime by contrast was ecstasy or *enthusiasmos.* These terms or, better, their equivalents, continue to play a role in the vocabulary of aesthetic appraisal. We speak of ourselves as "blown away" or as "knocked out" or "bowled over" or "shattered" by a work of art, and this goes well beyond finding ourselves enough pleased to judge it perfect. Reading Longinus caused the cultivated audiences of the eighteenth century to wonder why their art never lifted them out of themselves, which is what "ecstasy" means, and thus the idea of the sublime collided with the sphere of the tasteful as a disruptive force, much in the way the god Dionysus invaded Thebes in Euripides's unsettling play, *The Bacchae.* Grace and beauty all at once seemed paltry and insufficient. A recent commentator compared the impact of *On the Sublime* to that of Freud's writings on our own times. In proposing sex as the main drive in human conduct, Freud made everyone restless and emotionally uncertain, and feeling that in terms of orgasmic promise, something was missing from our civilized little lives. Think of Thomas Mann's character in *Death in Venice*. Beauty was a source of pleasure—but sublimity, in art and especially in nature, produced what Burke spoke of as "the strongest emotion which the mind is capable of feeling."

But what exactly was that feeling? In a review devoted to some pictures by the German Romantic painter, Caspar David Friedrich, in which one or more personages is shown from behind and gazing at the Moon, the *New Yorker* art critic, Peter Schjeldahl, expressed reservations on the critical usefulness of the term. The sublime, he writes, is a "hopelessly jumbled philosophical notion that has had more than two centuries to start meaning something cogent and hasn't succeeded yet." And he goes on, affecting a sublime historical cluelessness: "As an adjective in common use, the word is correctly employed not by Immanuel Kant but by Frank Loesser: 'The compartment is air-conditioned, and the mood sublime.'" Nothing that rocked an entire and largely self-congratulatory culture like the Enlightenment could have meant something so innocuously gushy. Here is a good example of how the term was actually employed in common eighteenth-century usage. Abigail Adams, in 1775, describes in a letter to her husband, the noise of cannons, which she observed from the top of Penn's Hill in Boston. "The sound I think is one of the Grandest in Nature and is of the true Species of the Sublime. 'Tis now an incessant roar. But O the fatal ideas that are connected with the sound. How many of our dear country men must fall?" The Sublime was in fact associated with fear in Burke's writing, and in some degree in Kant's, but mostly Kant treated it with reference to such feelings as wonderment and awe—words he uses in the Conclusion of his *Critique of Practical Reason,* in one of his most famous passages:

> Two things flood the mind with ever increasing wonder and awe [*Bewunderung und Ehrfurcht*], the more often and the more intensely it concerns itself with them: the starry heavens above me and the moral law within me.

So a piece of art would be sublime that elicits in a subject this complex mixture of wonder and awe. The German word is compounded of two morphemes, connoting deference and fear, though the latter is scarcely implied by its English equivalent. More than a feeling for beauty, the responsiveness to sublimity, Kant realized, is a product of culture. But it "has its root in human nature." It is part of what we are. Longinus too says something to this effect:

> We are (heaven knows) somehow driven by nature to wonder not at small streams, even if they are clear and useful, but at the Nile and the Danube and the Rhine, and still more at the Ocean; nor, of course, are we more astonished by that little flame which we kindle . . . than by the gleam of the heavenly bodies, though they are often gloomed over, nor do we generally consider it [i.e., the little flame] more worthy of wonder than the craters of Aetna, whose eruptions carry up rocks and whole mounds from the abyss and sometimes pour forth rivers . . .

Kant cites such examples in his discussion of the Sublime:

> Bold overhanging, and as it were threatening rocks; clouds piled up in the sky, moving with lightning flashes and thunder peals; volcanoes in all the violence of destructive hurricanes with their track of devastation; the boundless ocean in the state of tumult; the lofty waterfall of a mighty river, and such like.

My "native informant" from the eighteenth century, Abigail Adams again, used a precisely Kantian vocabulary when she embarked on her first ocean voyage to join her husband in Europe. Finally able to go up on deck after suffering sea-sickness, she noted in her diary, that she "beheld the vast and boundless ocean before us with astonishment, and wonder."

What is fascinating in Kant is that we are in the same way "driven by nature" to have a comparable attitude toward morality, which he explicitly characterizes in terms of the power or might "which it exercises in us," whatever our personal interests. Abigail Adams, in whom duty almost always trumped personal interest and inclination, would have accepted this totally. But where would we find a comparable power in art? Here Kant's experience was severely limited by what Newman speaks of as "the Renaissance imagery of individuals and objects." The art Kant knew was entirely representational, and though sublime things can be represented, they cannot be represented as sublime. This is one major difference between the beautiful and the sublime: the beautiful *can* be represented as beautiful. "The sublime of art is always limited by the conditions of agreement with nature," he writes, which restates the mimetic theory of art Kant takes as given. The mimetic theory rests on a congruity of boundaries, which is the condition of drawing. Kant specifies that "the beautiful in nature is connected with the form of the object, which consists in having definite boundaries." The sublime, by contrast, "is to be found in a formless [what Adams speaks of as "boundless"] object, so far as in it or by occasion of it boundlessness is represented, and yet its totality is also present to thought."

Consider the paintings of the artist, Vija Celmans, who does pictures of the starry heavens or of the ocean. These are paradigms of the sublime, since we know that what they depict are "boundless totalities." Yet we could not easily think of her paintings themselves as sublime, mainly because they do not elicit in us any special feeling of wonder on the scale that sublimity seems to require. And that in part is because of the scale of the pictures themselves, which one could hold in one's hands, as at a picture-dealer's. Somewhat closer might be the seascapes or landscapes exhibited recently at the Pennsylvania Academy as examples of "The American Sublime"—the paintings whose makers subscribed to the theory that God expresses himself in nature and does so with particular vehemence in those aspects of nature which have a certain grandeur. I refer to the so-called Hudson River School, which flourished in the mid-nineteenth century, and whose archetypically large-scale paintings featured nature itself at its largest—the Andes, or Niagara Falls, or the Grand Canyon. Such paintings perfectly illustrate Longinus's descriptions of the natural sublime, though I am uncertain whether there would have been paintings in his age which could have done so. There can be little question that the Hudson River artists reverted to large size in order to instill the awe and wonderment their depicted scenes aroused.

Kant, who of course never visited Rome, does speak of

The bewilderment or, as it were, perplexity which it is said seizes the spectator on his first entrance into St. Peter in Rome. For there is here a feeling of the inadequacy of his imagination for presenting the ideas of a whole, wherein the imagination reaches its maximum and, in striving to surpass it, sinks back into itself, by which, however, a kind of emotional satisfaction is produced.

I have often been struck by the fact that the original decorative program for the Sistine Chapel had the vault painted as the starry heavens above—which would in anticipation of Kant have had what went on in the chapel itself as "the moral law within," inner and outer reference giving an architectural embodiment to the two sublimities. Julius II wanted something more "modern" when he commissioned Michelangelo to decorate the vault—and the Sistine ceiling itself, I believe, is a good example of at least part of how the sublime works in art. It is so if we consider that the sublime belongs, if we may borrow Wittgenstein's expression, to "the world as we find it," without any prior or special knowledge. Let me explain by returning to the starry heavens for just a moment.

Neither of the great wonder-eliciting things that Kant writes about in the *Second Critique*'s Conclusion is "shrouded in obscurity beyond my own horizon." Rather, Kant says, "I see them before me and connect them immediately with my own existence." I stress the fact of immediacy in connection with the starry heavens, because Kant wants to say that if we are to speak of it as sublime, "we must regard it, just as we see it, as a distant, all embracing vault." *Just as we see it* means that we would see it as sublime no matter in what relationship we stand to the history of astronomical science. That is part of the reason that it belongs to aesthetics. In respect to its sublimity, we are on the same footing as what Kant would refer to as savages. So we must see the starry heaven the way anyone anywhere would see it, whatever their cultural condition. Kant of course had written on the nebular hypothesis, and even seems to have entertained a thesis about life on other planets. Thus he writes that if we regard the starry heavens as sublime, "We must not place at the basis of our judgments concepts of worlds inhabited by rational beings and regard the bright points, with which we see the space above us as filled, as their suns moving in circles, purposively fixed with reference to them." But sublimity has nothing to do with scientific thought.

To round the point off, this is what he says about the ocean as well:

> If we are to call the sight of the ocean sublime, we must not *think* of it as we ordinarily do, as implying all sorts of knowledge (that are not contained in immediate intuition). For example, we sometimes think of the ocean as a vast kingdom of aquatic creatures, or as the great source of those vapours that fill the air with clouds for the benefit of the land . . . To call the ocean sublime we must regard it as the poets do, merely by what strikes the eye.

Whatever, then, Kant may have meant by "the oftener and more steadily we reflect on *Der bestirnte Himmel*," he cannot have meant: "The more astronomical knowledge we acquire." The wonderment remains that of the poet and not of the scientist. The scientist, if anything, destroys the sublimity, the way Newton, to Keats's despair, unraveled the rainbow. "Science murders to dissect" was Wordsworth's putdown. The more we know, one might say, the less we feel. The mark of being in the presence of sublimity is, as with Stendhal, the swoon. If I remember rightly, there were female swooners at Gauguin's exhibition in 1888 in Paris. One gets a whiff of what the sublime must have meant in the eighteenth century when one reads Gauguin on the academic painters of his own time, who lived by the rules. "How safe they are on dry land, those academic painters, with their *trompe l'oeil* of nature. We alone are sailing free on our ghost-ship, with all our fantastical imperfections."

This is just how we feel when we first visit the Chapel to see the great work. Who understands what is happening up there? More important, one might say, who needs to understand it as far as the *sublimity* of the experience is concerned? The ceiling's restorer prided himself on getting as close as possible to "Michelangelo as artist and as man" by proceeding brushstroke by brushstroke across the vast expanse. But that is like the night-bird winging beneath the starry heavens. It gives it no sense of the circumambient sublimity. Neither, in fairness, does an image-by-image analysis of the ceiling, from the Creation to the Drunkenness of Noah. One does not need to know that program, tremendous as it is, to feel the sublimity of the painting. That feeling is importantly at odds with that kind of art historical knowledge which is on the same level as the theory of infinite worlds alluded to in the *Critique of Judgment*. So I take it then that this is what Kant has in mind with reference to "connecting [it] immediately with my own existence." And this in turn refers to his point about sublimity having to do with human nature and not merely with culture. The sublimity of things has nothing to do with special knowledge. Interestingly enough, this is analogous with something Kant says about the experience of beauty having nothing to do with bringing what we experience as beautiful under a concept. We find it beautiful before we know anything about it, as happened, in my own case, when I first saw one of Motherwell's *Spanish Elegies.*

In any case, Kant would not have known any example of sublimity in Koenigsberg, nor, given the Renaissance model with which he worked, could he have, though this requires a distinction. There is a sense in which he ought to have been able to imagine something that at least would be in candidacy for the sublime, and a sense in which he could not. He could not have imagined as art the kind of paintings Newman and Motherwell did. His position in the history of art limited his imagination severely. But he ought to have been able to think about artistic wonders, since the idea of wonders was certainly part of his culture. Let me discuss this briefly.

It is told of Michelangelo that he was seized with a remarkable vision in the course of several trying months spent in the marble quarries of Carrara, where he had gone in 1503 to select stones for the tomb of Pope Julius II. One day, his biographer Condivi tells us,

> He saw a crag that overlooked the sea, which made him wish to carve a colossus that would be a landmark for sailors from a long way off, incited thereto principally by the suitable shape of the rock from which it could have been conveniently carved, and by emulation of the ancients . . . and of a surety he would have done it if he had had time enough.

Michelangelo's inspiration was presumably the Colossus of Rhodes, one of the Seven Wonders of the ancient world—an immense sculpture, estimated to have stood more than 110 feet high, that according to legend straddled the mouth of a busy harbor. It was a wonder even when seen lying on the ground. "Few people can make their arms meet round the thumb," according to Pliny.

One tends to think of grace and balance, beauty and *disegno* as the paramount aesthetic virtues of Renaissance art, and indeed as marks of good taste in the fine arts well into modern times. But the idea of the colossus seems to belong to another aesthetic altogether, in which wonder and astonishment play the defining role. This other aesthetic was certainly embodied in the Seven Wonders themselves, and it inflected the great artistic figures of the sixteenth century, Leonardo and Michelangelo pre-eminently, who radiated, like some figure of ancient mythology, the aura of wizards. The colossus somehow emblematizes Michelangelo's visionary imagination, embodied in many of his signature works—the gigantic *David*, the immense decorative program enacted singlehandedly over the course of fifteen years across the Sistine ceiling, the tremendous vision of the Julian tomb itself, which, as perhaps the greatest sculptural commission of modern times, was to have incorporated more than forty large-scale figures. Leonardo's projected equestrian monument to Francesco Sforza was described by a contemporary as "the most gigantic, stupendous, and glorious work ever made by the hands of man." Leonardo worked on it over the course of fifteen years, and it stood twelve *braccia* high.

I have selected these colossi as paradigms only in part for the immensity of their scale, but mainly because, like the Seven Wonders—had the Julian Tomb been realized it would have been an eighth—they were meant to elicit feelings of wonder and awe, to which their scale contributes. Something is a colossus, for example, only because it underscores the limitations of those who experience it. It is perhaps in order to make visible the difference between themselves and their subjects that rulers have themselves represented as colossal, as in a seated portrait of Constantine the Great, thirty-odd feet tall, remnants of which still astonish when we see them in Rome.

But the idea of sublimity must entail something more than great size: "I attach little importance to physical size," the logician Frank Ramsey once wrote. "I take no credit for weighing nearly seventeen stone." So it is easy to understand why Kant—or Burke—felt that he had to add the sense of terror as the further condition. But Longinus's literary paradigms were the *Iliad* and a great poem of Sappho's, neither of which are terrifying. What they may do is remind us of our own limitations if we have artistic ambitions, and I think the feeling of wonder is connected with limitations in this way. "And still they gazed, and still their wonder grew, that one small head could carry all he knew," Edward Arlington Robinson wrote about a village prodigy. Kant brings these considerations into play in one of his formulations: "The sublime is that, the mere ability to think which shows a faculty of mind surpassing every standard of sense." I think the beauty of Helen of Troy was sublime in this sense. There is a very moving passage in Book III, where Helen leaves her weaving behind, and walks to the gates of Troy, to watch the warriors, who have paused for a moment before Menaleos, her husband, and Alexandros, her lover, fight over her. The elders of Troy were just then sitting in council—"And these, as they saw Helen along the tower approaching, murmuring softly to each other uttered their winged words: 'Surely there is no blame upon Trojans and strong-greaved Achaians if for long time they suffer hardship for a woman like this one. Terrible is the likeness of her face to immortal goddesses'."

We can imagine that someone was as beautiful as Helen, but we cannot imagine her beauty. That is one of the deep differences between words and pictures. In a related way, we can possess pictures of the Colossus of Rhodes, but no picture can show us its size. It can at best show us its scale, by showing a lot of tiny humans at its base, the way Piranesi did when he wanted to show the monuments of Rome as wondrous. But this brings us back to the limits of art as Kant understood it. Since sublimity is internally related to size, indeed to vastness, it cannot be pictured. That is one of the problems with Newman. The reproductions in a catalog of his characteristic paintings are incapable of showing their size, nor hence their sublimity. You have to be in front of and in fact rather close to them, in order to experience it. But again, terror is no part of the experience. My own sense, for what it is worth, is that the sort of vicarious terror Kant, and especially Burke had in mind, does play a role in human enjoyment—in ghost stories, horror movies, scary rides in amusement parks, in "cheap thrills," as it were. There may be cases where the experience of the sublime has terror as a component feeling, but it is not integral to the concept, in the way wonder itself is. After all, neither the starry heavens above nor the moral law within induce terror when we contemplate them. Parenthetically, fear continues to play its role in, of all things, the postmodern theory of the sublime developed by Lyotard, who speaks of the feeling in question as "an admixture of

fear and exaltation." One cannot but wonder—I at least cannot—
how often Lyotard can have had this feeling in front of works of
art. If it is like ecstasy, it cannot be something we can be overcome
by several times in a single visit to a gallery of art. My sense is that
Lyotard was overcome by the literature on the subject rather than
by actual aesthetic experiences he had had on the rue de Seine in
Paris.

It is difficult not to wonder, on the other hand, whether Kant
would have written the lyrical and romantic conclusion to the
1788 *Critique of Practical Reason*, in which he has recourse to an
aesthetic vocabulary and a set of relationships for which there is
really no place in the critical system as he had so far developed it,
had it not been for the concept of the sublime. The starry heavens
above and the moral law within can in effect be consigned to the
domains respectively covered by Kant's first two critiques—the
realm of nature, one might say, and the realm of freedom. And
these in turn are referred to the two great powers of the human
mind—to represent the world as a rational system, as covered by
universal laws; and to prescribe the laws which universally define
moral conduct. The philosophical portrait drawn by the first two
critiques is of a being at once cognitive and legislative. But it is not
an entirely adequate portrait if the concluding passage represents
part of our reality as human. Wonder and awe are feelings that do
not seem to belong to the somewhat austere, even severe person-
age the first two critiques would lead us to believe ourselves to be.
So we learn something fundamental about ourselves in contem-
plating our portrait that the portrait itself does not show. We learn
that we are not "pure intelligences" but creatures of feelings, and
not simply of feelings, but of powerful feelings, such as astonishment and awe. Small wonder, as we say, that a third critique had to
be written to connect us to the other two aspects of our being.
And since the capacity for wonder is disclosed to us in this striking
passage, the sublime—which is wonder's content—can hardly be
an afterthought in the *Critique of Judgment*. And the world as an
aesthetic presence is inseparable from what we are.

The Rediscovery of Man

Let us now return to Newman. There is a remarkable passage in
Kant that does bear on Abstract Expressionist aesthetics:

Perhaps the most sublime passage in Jewish Law is the commandment "Thou shalt not make unto thee any graven image, or any likeness of anything that is in heaven or on earth, or under the earth," etc. This commandment alone can explain the enthusiasm that the Jewish people in its civilized era felt for its religion when it compared itself with other peoples, or can explain the pride that Islam inspires.

This in effect prohibited Jews or Muslims from being artists since, though of course, like all the Commandments, it was and is violated in both religions. But until Modernism, there was no way of being a painter without making pictures. One could at best engage in decoration, which is the only alternative to picturing that Kant acknowledges. Paintings that are not pictures would have been a contradiction in terms. This in effect ruled out the possibility of making paintings that were *sublime*. But modernism opened up the possibility of aniconic painting, and this somehow brought with it the possibility of sublimity as an attainable aesthetic. As Newman said, "The Sublime is now."

Newman regarded his breakthrough work, *Onement I*, as a painting and not a picture. The catalog text to a major exhibition of Newman's work says that *Onement I* "represents nothing but itself"—that it is about itself as a painting. I can't believe that. I can't believe that what Newman regarded in terms momentous enough to merit the title, was simply a painting about painting. It is about something that can be said but cannot be shown, at least not pictorially. In general, the suffix "-ment" is attached to a verb—like "atone" or "endow" or "command "—where it designates a state—the state of atoning, for example—or a product. So what does "Onement" mean? My own sense is that it means the condition of being one, as in the incantation "God is one." It refers, one might say, to the oneness of God. And this might help us better understand the difference between a picture and a painting. Consider again the Sistine Ceiling, where Michelangelo produces a number of pictures of God. Great as these are, they are constrained by the limitation that pictures can only show what is visible, and decisions have to be made regarding what God looks like. How would one *picture* the fact that God is one? Since *Onement I* is not a picture, it does not inherit the limitations inherent in picturing. Abstract painting is not without content. Rather, it enables the presentation of content without pictorial limits. That is why, from the beginning, abstraction was believed by its inventors to be invested with a spiritual reality. It was as though Newman had hit upon a way of being a painter without violating the Second Commandment, which only prohibits images. Lyotard, incidentally, attempts to build the unpresentability of its content into his analysis of the sublime—but I think he had to mean that the sublime was *unpicturable*. Boldly post-modern as Lyotard took his aesthetic to be, it was curiously limited to painting.

Newman himself gave to one of his paintings the title *Vir Heroicus Sublimis,* which meant, as he explained to David Sylvester, "that man can be or is sublime in his relation to his sense of being aware." And it was his view, so far as I understand it, that he used scale to awaken this sense of self-awareness in relationship to his paintings: they imply, one might say, the scale of the viewer:

> One thing that I am involved in about painting is that the painting should give a man a sense of place: that he knows he's there, so he's aware of himself. In that sense he related to me when I made the painting because in that sense I was there. . . . Standing in front of my paintings you had a sense of your own scale. The onlooker in front of my painting knows that he's there. To me, the sense of place not only has a mystery but has that sense of metaphysical fact.

It is this "mystery," this "metaphysical fact," that scale and wonder evoke when we speak of the sublime. Scholars speak of the Renaissance discovery of man. We can, I think, accordingly speak of the rediscovery of man in Abstract Expressionism. But it is important that we recognize that we whose existence is implied by such paintings are not diminished, as we are by the starry heavens above. The scale of the painting is intended to induce a certain self-awareness, and this is what brings the status of sublimity with it. It implies the body of the viewer, without making us small because the painting is large. What Newman aspired to instill through such paintings as *Vir Heroicus Sublimis* is wonder and awe at ourselves as here. I cannot help but think that the concept Newman required was that of Heidegger's central notion, namely that of *Dasein*—of being-there and aware of being there.

But there is another way of thinking about this that I find magnificently expressed in an answer given by the great Russian novelist, Vladimir Nabokov, when an interviewer asked him if he was surprised by anything in life. Nabokov responded:

FIGURE 22   Barnett Newman, *Vir Heroicus Sublimis*, 1950–1951
  A sense of your own scale

The marvel of consciousness—that sudden window swinging open on
a sunlit landscape amid the night of non-being.

I find this passage sublime, and it is a matter of chagrin to me that
until fairly recent times, no philosopher has spoken of consciousness with this kind of wonder and awe. Certainly Kant did not. He
finds the starry heavens and the moral law within as matters of
wonder and awe without noticing that they pale in comparison
with the fact that he is aware of them, that the universe, inner and
outer, is open to something that is in itself unpicturable and perhaps even unintelligible, given the internal limits of human understanding. Small wonder philosophers took it for it granted—it
never became an object that had to be reckoned with in drawing
up the inventory of wonders.

Meanwhile, I note that Nabokov cannot forebear speaking of
something beautiful as the object of consciousness—a landscape,
sunny, and seen through a window frame. If consciousness disclosed only unrelieved disgustingness, we would wonder why we
had such an endowment. But this brings us back to the two worlds
of G.E. Moore that we considered early in our study. The world of
sheer disgustingness would not be one we would wish to be conscious of for very long, nor for the matter live a life that would lose
its point without sunlight. If I point to a painting of a sunlit landscape and pronounce it sublime, someone might correct me and
say I am confusing the beautiful and the sublime. I would cite

Nabokov and reply that the beautiful *is* the sublime "amid the night of non-being." Kant brings these considerations into play in the formulation we noted above: "The sublime is that, the mere ability to think which shows a faculty of mind surpassing every standard of sense." I might even, if feeling impish, add: It is sublime because it is in the mind of the beholder. Beauty is an option for art and not a necessary condition. But it is not an option for life. It is a necessary condition for life as we would want to live it. That is why beauty, unlike the other aesthetic qualities, the sublime included, is a value.

Index

Abject Art, 56, 57
Absolute Spirit, 136
Abstract Expressionism, 2–3, 20, 84, 85, 156; and aesthetics, 1,7
Achilles, 141
Adams, Abigail, 148, 149, 150
Adeimanthus, 75
Adorno, Theodor, 19
Aeschylus, xviii
aesthetics, 1–2; and beauty, 7–8, 59–60, 91; and black culture, 76–77; and ethics, 77; and feminism, 77; of photography, 82
aesthetic tourism, 81
Alberti, Leone Battista, 64
Alcibiades, 91
Alexandros, 155
Apollo, 142
Arensberg, Walter, 9, 94
Aristotle, 68; *Poetics*, 92
Arneson, Richard, 135
Arnold, Matthew, 28
Arp, Hans, 48
art: aboutness of, 65–66; and aesthetics, xxiii, 2, 7, 10, 58–59; as distinct, 94; as anthropology, 130; and beauty, xviii–xix, xxiii, 25–26, 29–30, 83, 95, 100, 110, 121, 122, 123–24; —as distinct, xix, 8, 14, 33–37, 45, 46, 58–59, 60, 88, 101, 107, 108, 119, 120, 145, 160; —inappropriate,

112–13; —internal, 112–13; to change society, 105–08, 119; concept of, xviii–xix, xx, xxi; —in ancient Greece, xvii–xviii; defining, xxiii, 6, 22, 25; defining itself, 20; and disgust, 50–52, 53, 59, 60; as embodied meanings, 139–142; end of, xxii–xxiii, 19, 136–37; history of, xxii; identity of, xxiii; and indiscernible pairs, 23–24; inflection in, 121, 123; as inner life, of culture, 128–29; institutional theory of, 24; and inwardness, 75–76; as knowledge, types of, 126–29; meaning in, 13; mid-sixties, xx; modern, 19–20, 120, 145, 146; —and Cold War, 26; and the museum, 62–63; 1960s, xx, 2–3, 14, 19, 20; philosophical definition of, xx; philosophical history of, xxii; and philosophy, connection between, 118, 137; philosophy of, xxii; pluralism of, xxiv; political, 103–04, 107–08, 119; and politics, 123; pragmatic properties, xix, xxiii; question of appropriateness, 118; radical openness in, 17–18; as rational and sensuous, 93; and real things, distinguishing, 64–65; semantic property of, xxiii; self-critique in, 19; and socio-